CU00970681

D —*Call It*— ELMARVALOUS

How to Talk, Cook, and "Feel to Hum" on "Thisseer" Delmarva Peninsula

Virginia Tanzer

EPM Publications, Inc.
McLean, Virginia

To Ward and Catherine

Call It
DELMARVALOUS

Library of Congress Cataloging in Publication Data

Tanzer, Virginia.
   Call it Delmarvalous

   1. Cookery, American—Delmarva Peninsula. 2. Del-
marva Peninsula—Social life and customs. I. Title.
TX715.T16 1983   641.5975   83-8880
ISBN 0-914440-69-0

Copyright © 1983 Virginia Tanzer
All Rights Reserved
EPM Publications, Inc.
1003 Turkey Run Road
McLean, Virginia 22101
Printed in the United States of America

Book Design and Illustrations by Hatley Mason

CONTENTS

FOREWORD

During the 1950s when my husband, daughter, and I lived in Washington, D.C., we used to vacation on the Delmarva Peninsula, sometimes on the Eastern Shore side, sometimes on the Atlantic side. Each visit found us increasingly charmed with Delmarva, and eventually we were able to live here year round.

Since we moved to the Peninsula, I have tried to capture on paper some of the qualities which make it unique. Articles about aspects of Delmarva have appeared in *The Delaware Coast Press, The Whale, The Delmarva News, Heartland, The Peninsula Pacemaker,* and *A Delaware Sampler.* My first book, *Seagulls Hate Parsnips,* celebrated the Delaware Shore area where we live.

My delight in Peninsulans' unique way of talking led me to try to record it in this book. I hoped thus to preserve it and other features of Delmarva culture before they vanish into the homogeneity which is obliterating regional accents and ways all around the country. Such an endeavor necessarily falls short of reproducing the charm and richness of the original. One thing is certain, however. The more exposure you have, the greater is your respect and admiration for the many facets of Peninsula life.

Virginia Tanzer

THE
SCENE

Chapter 1

UNIQUE LAND OF PLEASANT LIVING

Hundreds of books and articles have been written about the Delmarva Peninsula. At least two of these are famous and widely read—James Michener's *Chesapeake*, and Marguerite Henry's *Misty of Chincoteague*. In spite of these renowned publications and others, a large percentage of Americans have only the vaguest notions of the who's, what's, and where's of Delmarva.

Westerners tend to think that the Pacific is the only ocean around, that the world ends east of the Rockies, and that any landscape without mountains isn't worth looking at. Middle America concentrates on the Great Lakes, the Mississippi, Mark Twain, Detroit, and Marshall Field's. New Englanders believe that all U.S. history begins with the Pilgrims, that spring doesn't start until May, and that to describe a route from Boston to anywhere, all you have to do is indicate whether or not you go through Dedham.

Nevertheless, the Delmarva Peninsula does exist. It is a large (5,820 square miles), flat, watery area of tidewater country that is shared by three states—Delaware, Maryland, and Virginia—and includes 14 counties. It stretches south, like a pointing hand, 195 miles long, 70 miles wide at its widest, and less than 10 at its narrowest. Inhabitants claim, however, that the Peninsula's real size depends on whether it's low or high tide, for the place is awash in water, both salt and fresh.

Delmarva is entirely surrounded by water. The Chesapeake and Delaware Canal to the north actually makes the area an island, not a peninsula. To the west is the Chesapeake Bay; to the east the Atlantic Ocean and the Delaware Bay and River; to the south the opening from the ocean to the Chesapeake.

Not only is Delmarva surrounded by water, it is criss-crossed by water. If you were coloring a map of the Peninsula, most of the map would be blue, for in addition to the vast waters surrounding it, Delmarva claims an uncountable number of rivers, streams, branches, bays, canals, coves, swamps, guts, marshes, landings, and ditches. Just on the west side alone, 48 rivers run into the Chesapeake Bay, and there are over 3,000 miles of shoreline. The Peninsula is really water-logged. As someone has said, Delmarva is a place where water has meant much to many and something to all.

Because water has always played a dominant part in Delmarva's history, it follows that shipbuilding has also been very much part of life on the Peninsula. In the great days of the sailing vessels, towns such as Bethel, Delaware (now declared an historic district), were busy shipbuilding centers. Bethel produced the famous tall ships known as Sailing Rams. One of these, now named the *Victory Chimes*, still plies East Coast waters as a cruise ship. Over a period of 175 years, 250 large sailing vessels were built in the small town of Milton, Delaware. Milford, Delaware, also knew lots of shipbuilding, particularly during World Wars I and II. And, of course, builders on the eastern shore of the Chesapeake Bay gave birth to renowned Chesapeake workboats such as the Skipjacks, Bugeyes, Log Canoes, Pungies, and Crab Skiffs.

A bird's eye view of Delmarva should include not only the raising and marketing of poultry, one of the biggest industries on the Peninsula, but should also take note of another kind of feathered life that abounds on the Peninsula. Delmarva lies under the Atlantic flyway of migrating birds—song birds, game birds, and water fowl—all of which stop here on their way south. Many of the birds are here year round, and with the use of mechanical harvesters that leave more grain in the fields, the numbers of swans, geese, and ducks that winter here have greatly increased. The overwhelming feathered presence adds greatly to the interest, beauty, and diversity of life on Delmarva.

All by itself, this little stretch of land provides a cornucopia of goodies. We have here huge food producers, processors, packers, and distributors. Large numbers of hogs are raised, processed, and marketed. So many are there, in fact, that there is now an annual Delmarva Pork Congress, and a pork recipe contest. Scrapple and sausage factories thrive. One of the largest beef cattle feeding operations east of the Mississippi is located here, and Delmarva is the fourth largest chicken producer in the nation. Turkey farms also prosper. One large farming operation specializes in blueberries. Beekeepers and beekeeping associations abound. (Soy honey is delicious.) The rich Peninsula farmland produces mountains of peaches, sweet potatoes, watermelons, truck crops, corn, wheat, soybeans, and even tobacco. Farming is big business on the Peninsula. Add to that the seafood industry and tourism and you have the big money makers.

In spite of frequent feints and threats by heavy industry (mainly coal and oil), manufacturing on Delmarva has largely been kept to "clean" industries such as the DuPont nylon plant in Seaford, Delaware, and modular housing factories. Lumber, construction, and paper companies thrive here.

As a result, the air remains clean and sparkling all over the Peninsula. Pollution has not yet drastically affected its waters or its land. Wildflowers nod along every road and spread color across fields. Roger Tory Peterson called Delmarva one of the last great wildflower gardens on the eastern seaboard. And in spite of an increasing population and development, Peninsula farmland is still checkerboarded by large stands of trees. In autumn, the dark greens of the pines, cedars, and hollies are highlighted by the brilliant colors of the deciduous trees—sumacs, dogwoods, maples, and sweetgums. The bays and rivers have problems with pollution, it is true, but awareness of the troubles is widespread, and many organizations such as The Chesapeake Bay Foundation are attempting to find solutions.

It is also true that the Peninsula embodies one long trail of history. You might even refer to the area as an art gallery featuring 18th- and 19th-century houses. Famous indeed is the Maryland telescope style of architecture, with its high ceilings, outside chimneys, and one-room depth. Plantation houses in the southern, Virginia area are glorious examples of a gracious past. Victorian gingerbread mansions are scattered around Delmarva, with concentrations in Dover. In the spring, particularly, but also at other times of the year such as Christmas, house tours in all three states celebrate the life styles of bygone days.

The waters surrounding Delmarva have created one particularly colorful aspect of Peninsula life—the pilots' associations of the three states, whose members are responsible for the safe navigation of all ships entering the Delaware Bay and River and the Chesapeake Bay. All three organizations have a long history. Because navigation in both bodies of water is tricky, the pilots are regarded with the kind of awe afforded those whose work requires great skill and is sometimes perilous. Climbing a rope ladder to the deck of a super tanker in heavy seas is no mean feat in itself, and piloting ships through dangerous water requires constant vigilance, mental alertness, and great knowledge.

Because of its cultural homogeneity, the Peninsula should probably be one state, rather than divided into three bodies politic. There have often been half-joking moves to unite the Peninsula. Variations do exist, however, in temperature and climate throughout the Peninsula. The tip of the Peninsula, tempered by water on either side and by the Gulf Stream, has almost a month longer growing season than do areas in the north. Slight variations in speech also exist. There are those who claim, like Professor 'iggins, to be able to tell which county a person comes from just by listening to him talk.

The protective waters have made it difficult, until recently, to reach the Peninsula. This fact has contributed greatly to the retention of Delmarva's unique flavor, and to its ability to cling to its own way of speaking, cooking, and thinking. Now, since the arrival of better roads, ferries, and bridges, the surrounding megalopolis is pressing close, close, closer to this still fairly unspoiled land. Change is particularly noticeable in summer, when vacationers pour into the area by the hundreds of thousands, bringing with them many of the ills they are trying to escape. During the rest of the year, however, the Peninsula remains verdant and pastoral—a farming and fishing country that provides a rare link between the present and the past.

In this suspended time, the language of the Peninsula is spoken in the slow, soft rhythms of a vanished age. Native "barn" Delmarvans cling to the traditional ways of thinking and to their old-fashioned moral values. In these days of video games, pot, and punk rock, to be in backwater, backcountry Delmarva is like finding yourself in the middle of another century.

Chapter 2

RYE CHEER TO THISSEER PENINCHULA'S A RAHT TOLLABLE PLACE TO LIVE

It is a comfort to realize that Delmarvans have so far resisted all pressures from TV and increased mobility, and have clung to their own way of talking. The accent may vary from county to county, but overall the Delmarva way of speech is unique. Thank heaven for that. May Delmarvatalk never change.

Not that many Delmarvans realize their speech is different from anybody else's. They will laugh like crazy at stories about Swedes in Minnesota who say, "Wuryinia, Wuryinia, stop yumpin and yellin. It is going to raining." Or they marvel at regional accents such as that of Bostonians who "send their smaat children to baading skyules and then on to Have-id." Yet few Delmarvans realize that they themselves have a way of speech that often puts new arrivals into a blue funk of puzzlement.

"Ees win kum up airie arternoon," for instance, might well be Bantu or Swahili, for all a new arrival knows. In reality it is merely a Delmarvan's way of announcing that hereabouts an east wind blows every afternoon.

Some Delmarvatalk has been passed down from generation to generation since the first settlers arrived 350 or more years ago. "Airish," meaning cool or crisp weather, is listed by the *Oxford Dictionary* as an early English word. Ditto "pine chats," pronounced with a soft "sh." In much of the country, these are referred to as pine needles. "Housen" (houses) and "holpen" (helped) are two other words with ancient origins, probably Anglo-Saxon.

Delmarvans also do a funny thing with the word "anymore." They treat it as one word, and as if it meant "nowadays." Webster lists it as two words meaning "anything or something additional or further." In this sense, the words are usually used with a negative, as "I do not need any more." Ignoring this, Delmarvans will say, "Things costez so high innymore," or "The price a stamps is too high, innymore," or "Ah don know where the years go, innymore."

The recipe for Delmarva speech might be to take an Elizabethan accent, add a dash of Southern drawl, and flavor with Peninsula eccentricity. Delmarvatalk's peculiarities are most noticeable among those living in the remotest corners of the Peninsula. These peculiarities vary widely from one community to another. Farmers talk one lingo, watermen another. But even highly educated, broadly traveled Delmarvans talk about going "acrost to Balmur from the Easn Showar of the Peninchula."

Like that little taste? Listen.

"Airywhichaways you look at it, many a native barn Delwuryan, Murliner, or Virginnyan lives rye cheer to thisseer Peninchula. Prolly he thinks growin carn or beans, raisin howgs an biddies, or arsterin an crabbin urr the onliest way to make a livin innymore. Innyways else, he don know from a buncha beets. He putts a war fence aroun his feels so they won git spurled, an makes his hum to places lak Shaft Ox Corner, Bivalve, Black Howg Gut, Arster, Sockorockets Ditch, or Shad Landin.

"Wunst or twiced a day, summers, he goes a fur piece over to the far hall to git him a soda or a gingie ale cawz iss shore hot, innit? You cain't fault him fer that. An sometoimes, win he gits tarred an tuckered out, he gits hizseff a hard man an asts him to cut off the lectric, swizzle out the drain in the zinc, rake the pine chats, fix the hopper, or go up on the ruff an clean the chimley. Oh my dear! Wooden you think he might could uv done that hizseff, even if he war a lil wore out? Innyway, havin the hard hep picked him up a lil."

Talkin lak that be more catchin than the measles. Even iffn you wuz barn 3,000 miles off and growed up without the fowgiess idee ware the Peninchula war, purdy soon you hear yourseff talking bout ruffs and far halls.

Iss a Delmarvaddiction, thaas wot it be. An on the next page, thur begins a Delmarvaddictionary.

THE
TALK

Chapter 3
DELMARVA DICTIONARY

ACROST: On the opposite side of. "It costez a dollar an a half to go acrost the bridge."

ADMIRE TO: Desire to. "Ahd admire to be invited to the Homecomin."

AFORE: Before. "He talked up a storm afore Ah could git a word in edgewise."

AH: The 1st person singular. "Ah had em turn on the lectric."

AHOLT A: To get possession of. "Ahd shore like to git aholt a some money."

AHRNJE: A citrus fruit. "Jav yer ahrnje juice this marnin?"

AIR: A mistake. "Emma Lou made a turrble air wen she dint finish colletch."

AIRISH: Elizabethan word meaning cool, crisp weather. "She gits up late cawz it's too airish afore ten or leven o'clock of the mornin."

AIRY: Every. "She don go to town airy day."

AR: Possessive of the plural personal pronoun "we." "Thisseer Peninchula, ar hum, is the bestess place in the world."

ARFUL: Dreadful, horrible. "Ain it arful!"

ARL: The area you walk down in church or theater.

ARN: A heavy, metal instrument used in pressing clothes. "Ahm gonna git me a new-fangled steam arn."

ARNIN: To use the **ARN**. "She done a whole heepa arnin yestiddy."

ARNSTONE: Long-wearing crockery. "He bought hizseff a nice setta arnstone dishes when he wuz up to Chestertown."

ARSH: People who live in a country to the west of England. "The Arsh celebrate St. Patty's Day by wearin green hats, drinkin whuskey, and havin parades."

ARSTERMAN: One who tongs, dredges, or dives for arsters. "In 1982, there were 5,300 licensed arstermen in Murlin."

ARSTERS: Popular bivalves abundant in Delmarva waters. "In the 1980–81 season, 2,459,661 bushels of arsters were harvested in Murlin waters."

ARTCHITECK: One who designs buildings. "We dint git no hep from no artchiteck."

AXT: To inquire, question, or request. "Axt me no questions and Ah'll tell you no lies." Sometimes pronounced "AST." "Ah ast him to go to Howston, Delwur."

AYUG: The reproductive body produced by birds, chickens and reptiles. "They got some nice brown ayugs in, down to Butch's."

B

BAYDGE: A light tan color. "Sue Ellen bought herseff a new baydge suit."

BALMUR: A large city in "Murlin." "To git to Balmur, you go acrost the bridge. Caint take no ferry no more."

BALMUR ORALS: A well-known baseball team from "Murlin."

BAR: To take with the intent to give back. "Kin Ah bar yer frah pan?"

BARD: Past tense of bar. "Ruth Ann bard mah arn cause hers got bruck."

BARN: To be brought into existence. "The Martins urr all native-barn Delwurians." "Ah nivver heerd tail of that in all mah barn days."

BAYID: A place of repose. "Iss arter leven. Toime fer bayid."

BELONGS TO BE: Has a right to. "Them thur housen belongs to be rye cheer, not over thur."

BERL: To agitate through heat. To seethe. "Yer wadder's berlin."

BESTESS: A-one. "They wuz the bestess beaten biscuit Ah ever et."

BEST THING I EVER PUT IN MY MOUTH: An

expression of gustatory pleasure used by practically everybody on Delmarva (and in the South). "Anne Margrut's strawberry pah (frahd arsters, carn pone, griyuts) was the best thing Ah every put in mah mouth." Variations in accent sometimes result in "the bestess thing Ah ivver putt in mah mouff."

BIDDY: A baby chicken. "Them fellers raise lossa biddies."

BLUE CRAB: Famous denizen of Delmarva waters. Its name comes from the blue on its front legs, or arms. Blue crabs have two unique features: (1) the ability to swim as fast as fish, and (2) the softness of their skin after molting, which earned them the name of soft-shelled crabs.

The blue crab's Latin name, *Callinectes sapidus* means "beautiful swimmer, savory," which tells it all. The Pulitzer-prize-winning book about these crabs and the crabbers who catch them—*Beautiful Swimmers* by William Warner—is must reading for anyone wanting to learn more about the Peninsula.

BOB: A pointed, curved projection. "He putt a bob war fence clear arown his feels."

BOOSHUL: A bushel. "He got him a booshul a arsters."

BRUCK: Past tense of break. Also meaning to be out of funds. "Ahm sorry yer warshin sheen got bruck." "He shore bruck that hoss good." "Ah caint go over to Hairntun cawz Ah's dead bruck."

BUB: A detachable, incandescent lamp. "Thisseer laht needs a new bub."

BUCKRAMS: Crabs with semi-soft shells 24 hours after molting. After 72 hours, a crab once again has a hard shell.

BUGEYE: In spite of its name, a sleek, two-masted sailing vessel, another of the famous Chesapeake Bay workboats. "Bugeyes double as arster drudgers and cargo haulers."

BUSTERS: Peeler crabs just starting to molt.

CAINT: To be unable. "You caint fault him fer that."

CAM: Pronounced to rhyme with ham. Serene, unruffled. "Thisseer ocean's cam as a dish." "We went out in a slick cam."

CARD: A thin rope or electric wire. "That thur arn shore needs a new card."

CARN: A grain. "The missus berled carn onna cob fer supper." "The carn in the feels in tassel." "Ah bin a-settin an a-drinkin carn likker." You also have carn pone, a bread you have to larn to like, and carn bread which needs no larnin to enjoy.

CARRY: To take, transport. "Woodja carry me to the far hall?" "Ah got to carry the chirn to school."

CHERRY STONES: Clams up to 3 inches in length.

CHICKEN NECKERS: People, mainly weekenders and tourists, who fish for crabs using chicken necks as bait. Watermen are wont to refer to them as "No count chicken neckers."

CHILE: A young person of either sex. "Waddam Ah gonna do bowt that chile's lowance?" "That chile's room's six ways from Sunday. He otta clean it up hizseff."

CHIMLEY: That piece of a building containing smoke flues. "John built hizseff a house an putt up a chimley on the ees side."

CHIRN: Infants or young persons. "Lossa chirn git barn evvy year."

CLUM: Past tense of climb. "The boy clum the tree." "He clum to the top by workin hizseff to death."

COLLETCH: A place of "har eddication." "Both mah boys urr in colletch. Keeps me bruck."

COLT: Below normal temperatures. "It shore be colt out." "Colter than an ole maid's kisses, innit?"

COME ON TO: Arrive soon. "He'll come on to you then."

COMES: Gets. "It comes light arful early, thass fer shore."

COONT: Not to be able. "He wuz bruck so he coont pay iz taxes."

COSTEZ: To spend for. "Things costez so much innymore."

CRAB SCRAPER OR JENKINS CREEKER OR BAR CAT: A workboat used to drag a crab scraper trap through eel grass to get peelers and soft-shelled crabs. These boats are motorized, but have, as William Warner points out, a grace of line that speaks of former days under sail.

CRADLE CARRY: A term referring to the way a male blue crab carries the sook (female crab) before and after mating.

CRICK: A small stream of water. "Airy crick in the county got friz up."

CRINE: Weeping. "Ain't no yewst crine in yer beer."

CRISFEEL: Crisfield, an eastern shore town in "Murlin." "Taint a better harbor this side a Crisfeel."

CRITTER: An animal. "That thur pore critter's feelin porely."

CULLS: Crabs too small to be legal.

CULTCH: A hard surface for the spat (small "arsters") to attach to.

CUT OFF: To turn off. "Mur Sue, woodja cut off the lights, please?"

D

DELWURYAN: One who lives in "Delwur." "To be a real Delwuryan yer granpappy otta been barn in Delwur."

DEVOTED TO: Very fond of. A favorite phrase of Delmarvans, as well as of "Suthiners" in general. "Ahm devoted to Senator Wims (Williams)."

DINNER: A meal Delmarvans eat while the rest of the world eats lunch.

DINT: Not to perform. "He dint know her from a buncha beets." "He dint buy it special. Thass iz reglar Sunday suit."

DITCHUNAIRY: An interesting pronunciation of what Webster produced.

DJEVER: Have you ever. "Djever see sich a foine sweet pertater pah?"

DOUBLERS: Jimmies and sooks that are mating.

DOWG: Four-legged domesticated animal. "He hunts rabbits with iz hown dowgs."

DRONK: Drunk. "Ah aint nivver been dronk but wunst in mah hull lahf."

DROWNDED: To a Peninsulan, the extra syllable adds emphasis to this sorry state.

DRUDGER: An oysterman dredging for oysters. "He been a drudger all iz life."

DRUDGIN: On the Chesapeake, drudgin is to dredge for "arsters," permitted only from Skipjacks, which are sailboats. On the Atlantic side of the Peninsula, clammers in powered commercial vessels "drudge" for sea clams or surf clams. At the mouth of the Chesapeake, Virginia watermen "drudge" for blue crabs in winter, a practice deplored by Maryland watermen who fish for crabs in summer. To avoid the cold, blue crabs bury themselves in the bottom mud in the winter. Many of these are sooks, carrying eggs. Hence, there are many people who feel that all winter "drudgin" is endangering the crab catch.

DRUTHERS: Choice. "If Ah had me druthers, Ahd go to Yurp next year."

DUMPLINS: Mostly as in chicken 'n dumplins. "Theezeer dumplins ain't a tall lak raised dumplins which mos everybody eats out west an places. Theezeer dumplins are flat an slippery, kinda lak wide noodles, an they come to Delmarva from the Amish people up to Pennsylvania."

DUN: An auxiliary verb expressing accomplishment. "He dun went to Balmur."

DRAP: To let fall. Also drop-like candy or medicine. "Ah drapped me gorget (necklace) behine the chair." "Ah needs to buy me some cough draps."

EASN SHOWAR: The eastern shore of the Chesapeake Bay. In other words, the "Murlin an Virginny" sections of Delmarva. "Delwuryans" do not consider themselves part of the eastern shore, though they are proud to be part of Delmarva. The slogan "Land of Pleasant Living" was originally conceived to describe the "Murlin" shore, but definitely applies to the whole "Peninchula."

EES WIN: A wind from the east. "Ees win come up airy arternoon."

EITHER: Any, a single one. "Ah ain't caught either crabs today, innyways."

ET UP WITH: Consumed by. "Thatair man is plumb et up with hatin."

EVERYWHICHAWAYS: In all directions. "Ah looked everywhichaways fer Mur Ellen." Usually pronounced "airywhichaways."

FAHN OR FOINE: Fine. "Har you?" "Ahm foine."

FALL OUT: To be ill. "Our dowg fell out yestiddy."

FAR: A conflagration. A state of combustion. "We had a far in the far place an used oak lowgs." "The three wise men musta belonged to a Volunteer Far Kumpny cawz they kum from a-far."

FAR FLY: A nocturnal insect, a lightning bug. "There war a heapa far flies on the lawn lass night."

FAR HALL: "A place where farmen gather to foit fars. Also where the wives of farmen holt bake sales to raise money fer the far kumpny."

FARTHEREST: The greatest distance. "He stood the fartherest away as he could."

FAULT: To blame. "He jes admires to go fishin, you caint fault him fer that."

FAWNY: Funny. "How come you bin a studyin all those fawny things?"

FAVOR: To look like. "That chile favors iz daddy."

FEARD A: Afraid of. "Some folks are jes plain feard a the water. Iss nachurl wiff em. Ain't thur fault."

FEEL: Cleared land. "He planted iz feel in beans." "Hope we gits rain so there won't be no feel fars. Lass year bout this toime, Ahda lak to drown, there's so much rain."

FER: A preposition. "Ah looked fer it airywhichaways." Also means a long way. "Thassa fer piece away."

FLAR: A bloom or blossom. "Inna spring, the flars urr shore purdy." Also an aviator. "Elnor Ann shore be komplished flar."

FITTIN: Suitable. "Ahl be over tamar to fix the ruff if the weather's fittin."

FIXIN: About to. "He was fixin to go to Nappolis, but he change iz mine."

FORST: A large grove of trees, as in "The Black Forst." "Thurs lossa pine forsts on Delmarva, an airy spring youd a lak to sneeze yer seff to death from the pine pollen."

FOWG: A heavy vapor. "Thur war a heavy fowg over to Frankferd."

FRAHN: Cooking over a flame in a pan. "The chicken's frahn in the frah pan."

FRAH PAN: A skillet. "An arn frah pan is the bestess fer frahn chicken."

FREN: One not a foe. "He's shore bin a good fren to me."

FRENZ: Plural of **FREN**.

FRIZ UP: Frozen. "The crick dun got friz up."

FRUZ: Same as **FRIZ UP**.

FURRINER: Anyone who was not barn in "Delwur," "Murlin," or "Virginny."

FUTHER: Further. "The meat'll go futher if you slice it thin." "Those housen urr futher down the road."

FUST: Preceding all others; foremost. "His grandaddy was the fust mare of Crisfeel." Sometimes varied as "Fustess." "The fustess lady in the lan."

GIFF: A present. "It war a giff from Margrit an ain it purdy?"

GINGIE ALE: A soft drink. "Gingie Ale shore be tasty on a scorchin arternoon."

GIT: To obtain. To go. "Wheredja git that dowg?" "Ah gotta git over to Milferd."

GIT THE SMART OF OR GIT THE SMART A:
To learn. "Ah nivver did git the smart of it." "John, he bin tryin to git the smart a workin on the water."

GORGET: Necklace. "The gorget warnt his'n, it war hern."

GREEZEY: Oily. "Arter we cooked the bacon, the frah pan shore war greezey."

GRIYUTS: Ground hominy. "Nuthin better'n ham, griyuts an red-eyed gravy."

GROWED: Mature. "Six growed men axtin like kids." Sometimes accented with "full." "Ah kin drive the car now's Ahm a full-growed man."

GUV: To have bestowed. "Ah guv it all Ah got."

HAH TAHD: A period occurring "twiced each day win the ocean an bay waters reach a high point."

HAIRNTUN: Harrington, a town west of Dover, "Delwur," scene of the annual state fair. "He dun gone up to Hairntun to dinner with iz people."

HAR: To employ. Also, lifted up. "Ahm gonna har me nother man to hep in the feels. If you know as innybody good 'n all, leave me to know." Or "The balloon riz har an har." Or "We kint stan two more yars a har taxes."

HARD ATTACK: Failure of a hollow muscular organ. "Cassie Mae hadda hard attack jes afore Clumbus Day."

HARD HEP: Someone employed to help in house or yard. "She fed the hard hep dinner arter they putt the taters in."

HAR EDDICATION: Study at a college or university. "You don need no har eddication to work as a hard man."

HARRABLE: Simply dreadful. "Innit a harrable day?"

HAVE DONE: Have accomplished—always used without an object. "Lizbeth Ann, didja git aholt of Mur Ellen?" "Ah have done."

HEEPA: Lots. "That girl's inna heepa trouble."

HEERD TAIL: To gain knowledge of. "Ah ain't heerd tail of inny folk diggin fer arsters inna crick."

HEP: Assist. To furnish with relief. To prevent. "He hepped him win he war down an out." "He coont hep hizseff."

HERN: Belonging to her. "This feel a carn ain't his'n, iss hern."

HIS'N: Belonging to him. See **HERN**.

HIZSEFF: An emphasized version of the objective form of the prounoun he. "He shore got hizseff inna pickle."

HOLLER: A cavity in a solid substance. "He hadder in the holler of iz hand."

HOLP OR HOLPEN: Another pronunciation of help—a very ancient one which reaches back into Anglo-Saxon and Gothic. Holpen is the past tense. "Yestiddy, he holpen me with the hayin." "He cain't holp it iffn he warnt barn in Delwur."

HONGRY: Hungry. "Oh my blessed! Ah shore be hongry arter plantin mah feels."

HOPPER: The flush toilet. "They owney got one hopper over to the Smith's."

HOUSEN: Plural of house, the use of which dates back to Middle English. "On the Peninchula, iffn you don lak wur yer house is settin, ya move it. People urr always movin thur housen cause the land's flatter'n a runned over groun hawg."

HOWG: A swine, pig, sow, or boar. "That feller's very finnickety what he feeds iz howgs."

HUM: One's own domicile or place of abode. "Miz Truitt won' be hum til Sattiday."

HUNNERT: Ten times ten. "You awreddy dun tole me that a hunnert toimes." Also, "Delwur's" counties are divided into hundreds—hunnerts—a quaint political subdivision dating back to the early Anglo-Saxons.

HYEAR: Here. "They's a heepa folks kums over hyear summers."

IDA: I would have. Variation from "Ahda." "Ida gone myseff but it war rainin."

IMMEEJITLY: Right Away. "Ah'll be along immeejitly."

INNIT: Don't you think so? "It's shore hot, innit?"

INNY: No matter what one. "Jes gimme inny a them taters."

INNYMORE: Nowadays. "Things cost so high innymore."

IVVER: Ever. "Ah caint ivver fine him to hum."

J

JES: Just, simply, quite. "Ida jes as leave of kissed a mud turtle." "Ah's jes plumb tarred out."

JEVVER: Did you ever? "Jevver hear a sich a turble thing?"

JIMMY: An adult male crab.

JIMMY POTTING: A method of using a baitless trap containing two or more large male crabs which attract peelers (she crabs).

JINE: To join. "Reverend Foraker led the singin an we all jined in."

KAIRTS: An orange vegetable. "Kairts urr rut vegables lak pertaters."

KILT: Deprived of life, slain. "Iz dowg dun got kilt by a truck."

KIN: To be able. "Ah kin do it." Also, related to, as in kinfolk—synonymous with "people." "Ahm kin to her through mah mother's father's brother. They lives over to Wimmintun now."

KUMMUP: Rises. "Ees win kummup afore you could shake a stick."

KUMPNY: Guests. Or a firm. "Mis Purnell had kumpny fer supper." "He stablished iz own kumpny up to Millingtun."

LAK: To like or be liked. "Ah laks Lizbuth Ann a heap."

LARNIN: Acquisition of knowledge. "Ah don holt much with book larnin."

LAWNMORE: An instrument used to cut grass. "He bard mah lawnmore an nivver brung it back."

LEAST, LEASTWAYS, AND LEASTWISE: At least. "Least we're still tryin to fine the smallest car what they make." "He doin all raht. Leastways, he's doin the bestess what he kin." "Leastwise, my boat nivver scairt me."

LEAVE: To let, choose. "Leave us be!" "Leave us know how you come out." "Ahd jes as leave be in Toffit with a broken back."

LECTRIC: Electrical services. "Milferd don have no lectric cawz of the thunner starm."

LESSN: In case, so that. "Ahl putt yer gorget rye cheer lessn you fergit it."

LETTIN' UP: Becoming scarcer. "Church dinners urr lettin up aroun—frahd chicken dinners an all that."

LET ON: To show or display. "Don let on you see im."

LIL CRICK: A fishing village west of Dover, "Delwur." "There be a raht good restraunt in Lil Crick."

LISTEN AT: Imperative form of the verb "to listen." "Jes listen at all that hollerin. Lak to make a feller deef."

LITTLENECKS: Clams less than 2¼ inches long.

LOG CANOE: A famous Chesapeake Bay sailing vessel used for "arsterin" and hand "tongin." These crafts are very swift sailers and handle easily. They are now two, three, or even five logs wide. Log canoe races are a much-awaited annual event.

LOO-ESS: Lewes, a coastal town in "suthin Delwur." "Loo-ess be the oldess town in Delwur, stablished in 1631, but the fust settlers got kilt by Injuns."

LORDY GO TO FAR!: A memorable Delmarva exclamation. "Arr neighbor, Miz Chilcutt, won $50 at the races up to Hairnturn." "Lordy go to far! How'd she do that? She a expert or sumpin'?"

MAH OR MAHSEFF: Me, Myself. "Ahs gonna git mahseff a new picter fer the livin rum."

MAINESS: The most important. "The mainess way to keep yer parr more runnin good be ta oyrl it airy couple weeks."

MAKE A FAIR JAG: To earn a good living. "You caint make a fair jag arsterin win the prices is low."

MANINOSE: Soft-shell or steamer clams, many of which are sold to New England. Used both for the singular and the plural. For more information, see chapter 7.

MANO BOATS: Boats fishing for **MANINOSE** (soft-shell clams).

MARE: A city official. "Mare Kelley's been a raht good mare a Ocean City, feisty-lak."

ME: Possessive pronoun. "Ah shore hurt me knee."

MEER: A looking glass. "Heeza meer image of iz daddy."

MEGALOPS: A tiny crab, fully formed, but about the size of a large pinhead. In summer, swimmers are wont to complain that the "water fleas" are back. These causers of stings are not fleas, of course, but megalops, which, though tiny, can bite very well.

MEK: To make. "You mek a cake to bake it." Charming Delmarva inconsistency.

MENHADEN BOATS: Vessels using purse seines to fish for menhaden in the ocean, and which, by law, have been allowed to come within a half-mile of shore. Often confused with Trawlers or Draggers, which are not allowed within the three-mile limit.

MESSA: A quantity of. "She cooked up a messa turnip greens, howg jowls, and carn pone."

MIGHT WOULD OR MIGHT COULD: Be able to. "Mebbe it'll snow tmarra. Do you think it might would?" Or "We could set traps fer the mice. That might could be the answer." Or "I might could eat a cookie."

MISSUS: Always used with "the"; A wife. "Ah went hum to tell the missus bout it." **MIZ** is the pronunciation of "Mrs." "Good mornin, Miz Truitt. Howza baby?" **THE WIFE** is another way of referring to one's spouse. "The wife and Ah went down to Florida lass winner."

MOIND: To care, to care for, an inclination. "Ah dohn moind." "Wudja moind the baby fer a sec?" "Ah've a moind to go up town."

MOON PICTER: Movies. "Innit fun to go to the moon picters weekends?"

MOSTESS: The most. "He got the mostess peelers lass week."

MUFFLE: A covering to deaden noise. "That thur car dun got a real bad muffle."

MULTN: An historic town in southern Delaware named for the great English poet. In the 19th-century days of sail, "Multn" was an important shipbuilding center.

MUNGEM: In the midst of. "Thur warnt a honest man mungem."

MUNGYEW: All or some of you. Delmarva variation of y'all. "Mungyew better git raht on down heyah to putt out the far."

MURLIN: A state north of "Virginny" and next to "Delwur." Only a small part of it has the good fortune to be located on the Delmarva "Peninchula." The rest is west of the Chesapeake Bay. "Nappolis, the captul of Murlin," is on the western shore, "an a fur piece from the Peninchula."

MURRICA: A continent in the northern hemisphere. "Ahm shore glad to be Murrican."

MUSSRATS: See **RATS**.

NAPPOLIS: The "captul of Murlin."

NAR: The twenty-fourth part of a day. "How long's it take to git to Accomac?" "Bouta nar."

NARY NO MORE: Not any more. "Used to be we could getta heapa crabs by noon, but nary no more."

NEITHER: Not any. "He got neither crab today." "If we git neither crab today, Ahl give back the boat." "Ah don owe neither penny to nobody nohow."

NEKKED: Without clothing. "Thisseer city feller walked down the main street a town nekked as a jaybird."

NIVVER: Not ever. "Ah nivver had me a better toime."

NOHNDEED: Pleasant negative answer. "Do you think Ah need to git aholt of Jack?" "Nohndeed."

NOME: Polite way of saying no to a lady. "Have you fed yer dowg?" "Nome. Naw chet."

NOOKEELUR: A powerful explosive used in "lectric" plants an "war bums." "They otta putta stop to nookeelur bums."

NOT A HARDLY: Not in any way. "It ain't no life, not a hardly, livin aboard of a crab boat."

OF: About. "You been a studyin of arsters?"

OH MY BLESSED!: "Peninchula" exclamation. "Oh my blessed! What a racket!"

OH MY DEAR: Another strong Delmarvan expression of amazement, surprise, or dismay. The accent is on the "Oh." "Tmarra, iss gonna be colter 'n a jellyfish in January." "Oh my dear! The carn'll git friz up."

O-KORCHARD: A small town in "Delwur" on Rehoboth Bay.

OVER-TO: Peninsulans prefer "to" to "on" or "at." "He's over to Tangier." "She lives over to the western shore." "He's up to Milferd this arternoon."

OWNEY: An emphasis. For "alone" or "solo" see below. "If owney Ahda known aforehand."

OWNLIEST: Alone or solo. "It war the ownliest thing to do."

OYRL: A combustible liquid. "Mah bran new Chivvy awreddy needs a quarta oyrl."

P

PAH: A pastry dessert. "Hot dowgs an apple pah urr very Murrican."

PAPER SHELLS: Crabs 12 hours after they molt when the shells are beginning to harden.

PARR MORE: A motorized instrument used to cut grass. "Ah bought me a parr more yestiddy."

PASS THIS LAHF: To die. "Ira Sinclair passed this lahf lass Setterber."

PAY NO MIND: Pay no attention to. "Don pay that no mind."

PEELERS: Crabs that are ready to molt into soft shells.

PENINCHULA: Delmarva, the bestess place to live.

PEOPLE: Relatives. "She's to her people today." Used interchangeably with kin or kinfolk. "Mos evvybody got kinfolk all over thisseer Peninchula."

PERTATER: An edible, starchy tuber, also pronounced **TATER**. "Ah putt my taters in late this year." "The missus make a raht tasty white pertater pah."

PICK UP: Get better. "Charlie's bin feelin porely, but he picked up a lil yestiddy."

PICTER: A representation produced by painting, drawing, or photography. "The wife bought her a picter to putt inna livin room."

PIECE: A measurement. "The far house be jes down the road a piece."

PIHYUT: A cavity or hole. Also, a modern expression to mean the worst. "That shore is the pihyuts."

PINE CHATS: Pronounced "shats." Elizabethan word for pine needles.

PLAYCAKE: A flat bread eaten by some communities of Maryland watermen. William Tawes, in *God, Man, Salt Water, and the Eastern Shore*, writes that he was raised on playcake, black-eyed peas, navy beans, and pork salt side. Ingredients of playcake varied according to what was on hand—flour, shortening, yeast powder. Sometimes it was enriched with cracklings, when, Tawes says, it was the food of kings and gods.

PLUMB: Downright, absolute. "Ah plumb fergit to go to mah people in Hairntun arter the viewin."

PORE OR PORELY: Ailing. "He's feelin raht porely."

PREZINK: A gift. "Flars make a nice prezink win yer sick."

PROLLY: Probably. "Ah'll prolly go over to Return Day this year."

PRUFF: An established fact. "Do you need inny more pruff that thisseer Delmarva Peninchula is a raht tollable place to live or retar?"

PUTT: To place. "He hadda putt ayer in iz tars."

QUAHOG: A hard-shell clam found along the eastern coast and in Delmarva waters. For more information, see chapter 7.

R

RAHT: Opposite of left. Also used adverbially for "very." "How ya feel?" "Foine. Raht pert an tacky lak, in fak."

RAHT SMART: A lot of, or rapidly. "Ah caught me raht smart a crabs." "Thatair crab kin go long raht smart lak." "It's raht smart a line."

RATS: Muskrats, considered by many Delmarvans to be a great delicacy. "Ahl cooked me up a rat stew fer supper."

REST YER COAT: A form of greeting by having your coat removed. "Come in an rest yer coat a while."

RETAR: To cease working. "Lossa folk lak to retar on Delmarva, isso durn pleasant thur."

RICHMUN: The capital of "Virginny." "Lak Nappolis, issa fer piece from Delmarva."

RINCH: Rinse. "Ruth Ann! Go rinch them dishes afore they get all stuck up."

ROIT SMAHT: Variation of **RAHT SMART**.

RUFF: The cover of a building. "He clum on the ruff to fix the chimley."

RUSTLE OFF: Hurry. "He rustled hizseff raht off to see iz people."

RUTT: Root. "It shore war hard to git them rutts out. Tuck two stixa dynamite."

RYE CHEER: Right here in this place. "Rye cheer, not thur, is the bestess place fer a biddy house."

S

SARR: Opposite of sweet. "Oh my dear! That shore is a sarr pickle."

SARRUN: Warning noise made by a "far injun." "The sarrun woke evvybody up at 4 o'clock this mawnin."

SEBBYVILLE: Selbyville, a town in "suthin Delwur."

SHE CRABS: Young, female crabs.

SHEDDING FLOATS: Enclosed areas where crabs are put to molt.

SHORE: Assuredly. "That shore war a nice prezink fer yer mom mom and pop pop." (Delmarvans' way of referring to grandparents.)

SKAIRT A: Afraid of. "If a waterman's skairt a water, he better look fer some other kine a business."

SKEETER: A stinging insect. "Them skeeters lak to et me up."

SKIPJACK: A flat-bottomed, square-sterned working sailboat distinctive of the Chesapeake Bay. Named after a variety of fish which leap out of the water and skip over the waves. At the turn of the century, these boats were developed in Somerset County as crab and oyster boats. Skipjacks, along with Log Canoes, Bugeyes, Pungies, and Crab Skiffs are considered by many to be the most beautiful and elegant workboats in the world.

SODA: Any soft drink. "Ah lak all sodas, but mosely cokes."

SOFT-SHELL CLAM OR MANINOSE: A long-necked clam of the eastern coast popular for steaming. For further information see chapter 7.

SOFT-SHELLED CRABS: Blue crabs in the process of growing. In order to grow, blue crabs shed their shells, a process called ecdysis. Soft-shelled crabs are crabs in between hard shells. These are eaten whole and considered to be a great delicacy.

Soft-shells are rated by size: MEDIUM—3 to 3½ inches across the body; HOTELS—3¼ to 4 inches; PRIMES—4 to 4½ inches; JUMBO—4½ to 5 inches; WHALES or SLABS—5 inches or better.

SOOKS OR SOOKIES: Female crabs who have molted their exoskeletons for the last time. Adult female crabs have bright red pincers, blue claws, and olive green top shells. Watermen say, "Sooks an jimmies urr pickin crabs."

SPAT: Small **ARSTERS**.

SPECK: To suppose. "Ah speck he'll go over to Richmun ifn he gits lected."

SPICKET: A faucet in the "zinc."

SPONGE CRAB: A female crab carrying an extruding egg mass.

SPRIZE: Something unexpected. "Ah war so sprized you coulda knocked me over with a goose feather."

SPURLED: Decayed, or over-indulged. "The carn in ar feels got spurled by too much rain." "Tha thur chile is so spurled he needs to have a good thrashin ware he sets down."

STARM: A disturbance of the atmosphere. "We dun hadda bad thunner starm lass night."

STORE BOUGHTEN OR STORE BOUGHT: Not homemade. "Them rag rugs look hum made, but thur store boughten."

SUMMERS: Some place. "That thur hammer jes gotta be hereabouts summers."

SUPPER: A meal eaten in the evening. "Whyntcha come over to supper tonight?"

SURF CLAM: An East Coast clam which grows to 7 inches in width. For further information, see chapter 7.

TAKES: Brings. "What takes you here?"

TAMAR: The day after today. "Ah wunt buy that thur kine-a jeans, Mur Selma. You'd jes be throne yer money away. Whyntcha wait til tamar win we'll be over ta Wimmintun?"

TAR: A pneumatic apparatus covering a wheel. "Long bout Christmas is the toime to putt on yer snow tars."

TARD OR TARRIN: Exhausted, exhausting. "He felt arful tard arter he got through plowin iz feels." "Thassa tarrin occupation."

TAWMS OR TOIMES: Periods when something occurs. "Ah saw him a coupla tawms (toimes) afore he moved to Pokomoke."

TERECKLY: Soon. "The hard man'll be thur tereckly, God willin an the crick don rise."

TESTIFOY: To testify. "Ah'll testifoy to that. They done the bestess what they could."

THATAIR: That thing there. "Thatair hoss got the bad heaves."

THATAWAY: In that direction. "The bean feel is thataway, up thatair road."

THAT AH DO: A phrase of assent. "Thassa good price fer yer arsters, doncha know it?" "That Ah do. That Ah do."

THEEZEER: These things here. "Theezeer soft-shells urr the bestess Ah ivver seen."

THESSELVES: Themselves. "God heps those what hep thesselves."

THEY'S MANY AS: There are many who. Another idiomatic usage frequently heard on the Peninsula. "They's many as don lak it thatta way." "They's many as don know the right of it."

THISAWAY: Opposite of **THATAWAY**.

THISSEER: Something "rye cheer, not summers else."

THREW A WRINKLE: Stumped, surprised. "Oh my dear! You shore threw a wrinkle at me that tahm."

THRONE: Present participle of throw. See use under **TAMAR**.

THUR: Not "rye cheer."

THURSEFF: Another way of saying themselves. "They dun built thur hum thurseff."

TO: As in "Ahl have her to call ya." An interesting archaic use of the pure infinitive verb form often heard on Delmarva, which probably dates back to early English.

TOLLABLE: Tolerable, not bad. In fact, pretty good. "Ah got a tollable mount fer them biddies."

TONGIN OR RAKIN: Processes used to gather "arsters." The tongs, which have rake-like ends, traditionally have been operated by hand as the tonger leaned over the side of the boat, an exhausting process. Recently, hydraulically powered tongs have been allowed in certain areas of the Chesapeake.

TRIPLE NEGATIVE: A Delmarvan's method of emphasizing a point. "Aint nobody knows nothin about crabs nohow."

TROT LINE OR TROTLINING: A method of fishing for crabs which is probably the oldest form of crabbing—long lines with short baited lines tied to them at 3- to 4-foot intervals.

TUCK: Past tense of take. "He tuck and bruck it afore me eyes."

TUCK DOWN: To remove and lower. "He tuck down the bob war fence."

TUCKERED: Exhausted. "Ahm plumb tuckered." Or used with "out." "She gits tuckered out arnin."

TURKLE: Turtle. "The onliest way to pronounce turkle is turkle."

TWICED: Two times. "Not wunst, but twiced."

U-V

URR: Are. "Them thur biddies urr white leggerns."

UVVA: Beginning of a prepositional phrase used with certain nouns such as "slow." "Too slow uvva game." "She larned so much in that small uvva toime."

VEGABLES: Herbaceous plants cultivated for food. "Vegables lak kairts as lotsa viemin C."

WALD: Savage, stormy. "Ah shore went to a wald pardy lass night."

WANT: Wasn't. "It want a decent thing to do."

WAR: A thread of metal. "He got hizseff a bob war fence runnin clean arown the house." Also, a past tense of the verb "to be." "Thatair boy nivver war no good."

WARE-IVVER: Whatever place. "Ahda lak ta git aholt a that thur feller, ware-ivver ez at."

WARNT: Was not. "It warnt the raht thing to do."

WARSH: To cleanse by ablution; something cleansed. "Miz Talbot putt a big warsh in."

WARSHIN SHEEN: An appliance to help cleanse by ablution. "Margrit Ann dun bought herseff a new warshin sheen over to Monkey Ward's."

WARSHTUN: The nation's "captul."

WEARAT: At what specific location. "Thur's a wunnerful new restraunt in Cambridge." "Oh? Wearat?"

WHALES: Largest size of soft-shelled crabs.

WHOLE NOTHER: Be one different. "Thassa whole nother kittle a eels."

WIMMINTUN: Wilmington, a large city in "Delwur."

WIMS: A last name. "Senator Wims of Delwur wuz a moity fahn man. They calt him the watch dowg of the Senate." In the singular, the first name. "Wim Tell shot a arrow offn his chile's head."

WIN: At the time that. "Win did the far start burnin?"

WOODEN: Would not. "They wooden do it lessn they wanted."

WORE OUT: Exhausted, very "tard." "Pickin carn in thisseer heat's got me wore out."

WRAPPED UP: Covered with. "Ma car shore be wrapped up in dust."

WUNNER: A cause of surprise or astonishment, a miracle, or to feel doubt. "Issa wunner he dint git kilt." "Ah wunner if Christmas'll ivver git here."

WUNNERFUL: Extraordinarily nice. "Wotta wunnerful sprize to see ya."

WUNST: One time. "Wunst upon a toime."

Y-Z

YE: Second person singular. "Wanna be a scraper, do ye?"

YESTIDDY: The day before today.

YEWST: Use. "Ah aint got no yewst for that thur no-count feller."

YONDER: At a distant place. A quaint word often still used by Delmarvans. "The housen be half a mile yonder."

YURP: A continent across the Atlantic Ocean. "They tuk a trip to Yurp lass year."

ZATSO: Polite comment on hearing a piece of news. "This ain't bin a real good year fur beans." "Zatso?"

ZINC: Shallow vessel in the kitchen connected to a water supply and drain. "Sucha lotta dirty dishes. We'd best rinch em in the zinc."

Chapter 4

Mawnin Ma'am—A Sampler of Delmarva Talk

Mawnin, ma'am. Yer furrin to these parts, aincha? Well, yer welcome. Set yerseff down. Wozzat? You'd lak to know about thisseer farm? Well, okay. Ah don moind.

Me and Mur Sue, Mrs. Burton, we run this farm. Mah name's Layton Burton. Layton Rodney Burton's mah hull name. All three urr ole names hyearabouts. Lossa Laytons an Rodneys on the Peninchula. They been aroun since afore the Revlution. Cum over from Englan. Burtons, too.

You kin esk questions, if you want. Ah kin whittle an talk at the same toime.

Nome. Thisseer ain't no new farm. Ahm plantin an ploughin the same feels as mah father, an iz father afore him, owney now iss easier with tractors instead a horses an ploughs. Iss a good lahf, slow an easy lak, mosta toime. Essept win the weather sets up a hoorah an hoorangle. Sometoimes it rains dogs an cats an hammer handles. Other toimes iss drier'n a duck's back inna dessert.

Sometoimes, Sundays mosely, Mur Sue an Ah, we have kumpny to dinner arter church. Then she stirs up a messa chicken an dumplins. You don need no har eddication to know they is the bestess things you ever putt in your mouff.

Onliest thing is, mah missus be a foine woman an a hard worker, but she don admire to git up afore 7 urr 8 in the mornin lessn she's in the mood cawz iss too airish then. Almost airy day, arter she does git up, she turns on the wadder spicket inna zinc, rinches the dishes, then putts inna big loada warsh. Arter she tucks the close down, she still has the arnin to do. Lossa work, she says. That it is. That it is. Lahf's lak that, innit?

Wunst inna while, the wife and Miz Maull, ar neighbor, they admire to rustle thesselves acrost the bridge to Balmur, about the furtherest away they lak to git from hum. Lass Settermber, Mur Sur wanted to git herseff a nice setta arnstone plates. When she cum hum, her frenz wuz et up with green envy over them fancy store bought dishes. Ed Maull, he'd a lak to uv gone up to Balmur hizseff an watched the Balmur Orals play, but he war feelin porely, the dog fell out, and his secon cousin up to Harmony got kilt huntin 'rats, so Ed hadda go up thur to iz people. It war so fowgy, he said he's a lak to nivver got thur, not a hardly.

Later, the feller wot lives two, three housen down a road cum over, an arter a lil argyment, barred mah parr more. Ahd jes as leave be kissed by a mud turtle as loan him innythin again fer he tuck an bruck it. Ah axed him to be keerful, but he warn't. He's a full-growed man, too, and otter uv knowed bettern that. If Ah wuz him, Ahd been so shamed Ahd a crawled inna hole an pulled the hole in arter me. Hope to mah nivver, thass all true. They's many a folk wooden loan that thur feller nuthin no more, no how.

Oh my dear! Nome. Ah dint cut mahseff. Jes thinkin aboot that air no count feller, Ah guess.

Well, lak Ah say, it aint all hard work, thiseer farm. Mos evvy Thanksgivin Mur Sue an Ah, we go over to Crisfeel to visit mah people. Mah brother, he's a waterman an wooden wanna be innythin else. Keeps on goin through main strenth an awkardness. Sometoimes, he don get either crab all day. Don seem to bother him none, though. Crabbin an arsterin in a smaat breeze iz lak sittin inna rockin chair to him. Me, when the wind comes up rough an that boat starts bouncin aroun lak a buckin mule, Ah don feel too good.

Well, Ah guess it's lak they say, if yer barn to hang, you'll nivver git drownded.

Looka that. Howya lak that thur duck Ah whittled whilst Ah wuz talkin? Almoss lak a honess ta gooness mallard, innit?

THE
FOOD

Chapter 5

MUSSRAT STEW, ARSH PERTATER PAH, GRIYUTS, AN' THINGS

The fact that for hundreds of years the Delmarva Peninsula was hard to reach kept Peninsula speech and customs from becoming a TV-directed monochrome, but did not in any way keep Delmarvans from developing a superlative cuisine. It may not be "haute" or uptown, but it "shore war good."

Some Delmarvan recipes originated from the Peninsula's abundant foods such as blue crabs and oysters. Other delectables drifted up from the south, for the Peninsula is strongly southern in heritage and customs. "Murlin" and "Virginny" are solidly southern states. "Delwur" is more northern in its accent, but many people in its southernmost county, Sussex, are very southern in their leanings. Indeed, during the Civil War, residents of the county seat, Georgetown, were wont to fall upon each other in fierce combat over their northern or southern viewpoints.

Delmarvans cook up all kinds of southern delicacies, from spoon bread to beaten biscuit to "Murlin frahd chicken" to "karn pone." When used with the word "beaten" the word "biscuit" is rarely used in the plural. Plural or singular, beaten biscuit is something you have to learn to love. This cracker-bread-hardtack has been called "Delwur," "Murlin," or "Virginny" bullets, a nickname which tells all.

A state to the north, Pennsylvania, has also influenced Delmarvan cooking. Many Amish people originally from Pennsylvania now live around Delmarva, and they have contributed their own unique recipes. "Slippery dumplings" are one such anomaly, and can come as a distinct shock to "furriners" who order chicken and dumplings expecting little fluffs of dough in gravy. "Slippery dumplings" slide around in lots of gravy, all right, and are greatly relished by Peninsulans; but instead of being fluffy they are as flat as the Peninsula itself.

Scrapple is another Pennsylvania-inspired product now manufactured widely in "Delwur and Murlin." Maybe you live in one of those deprived areas, like the West and New England, where scrapple isn't available. Otherwise, you know the delights of scrapple and scrambled eggs for breakfast. This combination served with batter bread, for instance, is, if not heaven, at least cloud nine. For other ways to use scrapple, see the recipes under Pot Luck.

Serving sauerkraut with turkey is uniquely "Murlin," and a superlatively tart accent to the rich bird. In chapter 10 is a recipe for sauerkraut with apples, brown sugar, and onions that ought to make a devotee out of even the sourest sauerkrautophobe.

Until recent times, when the poor diamondback terrapins got to be scarcer than crocodiles on Delmarva, terrapins enjoyed a favored place on Peninsula tables. Way back when, people used to "go turklin." Old-time residents tell of their grandfathers having terrapin cellars, where the unlamented reptiles were kept on a bread and water diet until the household decided to put terrapin soup on the bill of fare. Some old-timers still put snapping turtle steaks in their freezers, but these tidbits, like 'possum and eel, are not to be found on most dinner tables. Other wild game animals and birds—deer, geese, and ducks—are far more popular.

The famous Chesapeake Bay and Chincoteague oysters are very much part of Delmarva life. As is true all over the country, they are eaten in every known way from live to breaded and "frahd." Perhaps unique to this area is the custom of serving "frahd arsters" with chicken "salat," an inspired combination never dreamt of in the West.

To prove a point about Delmarva's oyster opulence, there are a number of places on the Peninsula named after shell and fin fish—Oyster, Virginia; Bivalve, Maryland; Oystershell and Shelltown on the Pocomoke; Shad Landing, Virginia; and Cherrystone Inlet, Virginia. No better way to advertise the local goodies. There is even an Oyster Museum on the barrier island of Chincoteague.

Shad and shad roe, two more tasty treats, are very much part of Delmarva spring living. A wild, white-flowered bush—the Shad

Bush—is named after the spring shad run, when the fish return to spawn in home waters.

It used to be the custom to fish for shad just before Easter, then to enjoy shad roe and scrambled eggs for Easter breakfast and baked shad for Easter dinner. Alas, shad, too, are harder and harder to get. It stands to reason that if you eat up all the roe every spring, there won't be any shad the next year.

Blue crab is another delicacy that is becoming scarce. Dishes made from blue crab, such as crab cakes and Crab Imperial, are indigenous to this area. West Coast gourmets do not generally think along crab-cake lines, nor do they enjoy soft-shelled crabs, a great Delmarva treat, and certainly they have never heard of maninose, the soft-shell clams.

Other Delmarva specialties include Beach Plum Jelly and Liqueur, and Fish House Punch. Grits ("griyuts") are particularly delectable when served with turnip greens, "Murlin" ham and red-eyed gravy. There are sweet potato pies and biscuits. Even more typical of the area is white potato pie, the latter made from what Delmarvans call "arsh pertaters or taters."

We used to own a wonderful old (1690) house near Chestertown, Maryland. When we bought it, a big family of fine black people lived there. Just before settlement, we went out to the house to check a few things. In the old-fashioned sink were large buckets of greens to be washed and sorted. On tables in one corner were dishpans full of chicken pieces washed and floured for frying. On another table in the center of the big kitchen sat two large bowls. In the first one was mounded a delectable heap of hot mashed potatoes topped with melting butter. In the next bowl were deep orange, beaten eggs. As we watched, the mother of the family added seasonings and poured the eggs over the potatoes. Then she spooned the rich custard into pie shells.

Meantime, a daughter started frying the chicken. The smells and sights of that meal in the making had us in a near frenzy of taste anticipation.

No discussion of Delmarva foods should ignore muskrats. In Quantico, Maryland, the members of St. Phillips Episcopal Church put on an annual turkey and muskrat supper. You might like the recipe for your next big party. It comes to you courtesy of an article by Orlando Wootten in the 1980 spring issue of *Heartland,* a publication devoted to the Delmarva Peninsula.

"Here's how you cook muskrats, Quantico style. It turns out to be a sort of stew, a bit of argument here, for there are those who like the meat firmer. But Quantico style is, has been, and ever shall be. Take 500 muskrats, wash clean, cut up. Place the pieces in water in pots, bring to a boil, boil for 20 minutes, drain. Wash the meat off in warm water, scrub the pots, place the meat back into the pots and cover with water. Add much seasonings—sausage or bacon grease, salt, black and red pepper, and sage. Cook for three to four hours, until the meat is just about ready to fall off the bones. It is dark meat, a bit gamy.

"You, visitor, just eat it, don't say a word. Look straight ahead, eat it, and smile. Cross your fingers and say, 'Man, that's real eatin. I was weaned on 'rat meat—sure is good to be back to it.' At least that's what everyone else is saying. Don't let them get ahead of you. There's also plenty of fine, sliced white turkey meat with dressing and cold turnips, and a tank load of coffee—plus the best corn bread."

There are those who say that this is one of the epicurean delights of the world. Why not? Who wants caviar when you can have shad roe? Who needs Viennese Torte when there is Syllabub, that gorgeously fattening delectation of whipped cream, sugar, sherry, almond flavoring, and sponge cake?

Delicious, distinctive Delmarva dining! Pure Peninsula pleasure!

Chapter 6

PEELERS, SOOKS, JIMMIES, AND OTHER DELIGHTS

It is almost impossible to think about Delmarva without also thinking about blue crabs. On the West Coast, the Dunganess crab is considered the most delectable edible. On Delmarva, the blue crab is gustatory king. Its name comes from the blue on its front legs, or arms. Two qualities contribute to the blue crab's distinct personality—its ability to swim fast, as fast as a fish; and the extreme softness of its new skin after molting, thus producing the soft-shelled crab. The blue crab's Latin name, *Callinectes sapidus,* means "beautiful swimmer, savory," and seems to express the delight Delmarvans and others take in this crustacean.

Soft-shelled crabs and picked, packaged crabmeat both come from blue crabs. Small blue crabs that have molted their old shells in the process of growing are called soft-shelled crabs until the new shell has hardened. Picked crabmeat comes from the large, hard-shelled crabs, either male or female (jimmies or sooks).

Miles of printed words have appeared about the blue crab—how it reproduces, how it migrates, how it makes love, how to catch it, how to open it, how to eat it—all appropriate recognition for a crab that comprises 50 percent of the national crab catch.

Delmarvans have been fishing for blue crabs ever since anyone can remember. Interestingly enough, however, the use of blue crab meat, which is a favorite today for such things as crab cakes, is a fairly recent development. This meat is picked from large hard-shelled crabs—both female and male. But, as William Tawes pointed out in his *God, Man, Salt Water, and the Eastern Shore,* the picking and eating of the large jimmy crabs became popular only in this century. In the late 19th century, "the almighty crab was the summer God of the Creek watermen," but this referred largely to soft-shelled crabs. The large, hard-shelled jimmies and sooks were thrown back in the water. The current popularity of meat from jimmies and sooks has caused blue crabs to vie with Maine lobster for a place on the menu.

On Delmarva exists a whole vocabulary relating to the blue crabs themselves, to the backbreaking work of catching them, and to the kinds of boats used. The word "waterman" itself is peculiar to the shores of the Chesapeake. Among other words most Delmarvans take for granted but which are largely unknown elsewhere are: megalops, soft-shells, peelers, she crabs, doublers, busters, paper shells, buckrams, sponges, jimmies, and sooks. For definitions of these Delmarvawords, see the Delmarva Dictionary.

This list is only a beginning. The special terms relating to Delmarva fishing stretch to infinity. If you are listening to a waterman discuss these matters, the difficulty of understanding the special terms is compounded by the waterman's speech itself. Few landlubbers can grasp even half of what watermen are talking about.

Lots of creatures molt, insects as well as crabs. Blue crabs shed their exoskeletons many times during their lives. Male crabs shed 15 to 20 times, for instance. The molting process is an exhausting one for the crab, often taking three to four hours. The crab literally backs all of itself out of its old shell. After that the crab is helpless and ready prey not only for man but also for herons, cranes, bluefish, and other crabs. This makes it easy to understand why, although a female crab carries one to two million eggs, only one egg out of every million will produce an adult crab.

Experts say that the greatest amount of shedding takes place during the summer in the early morning hours, a week before the full moon, or one hour after high tide. Particularly difficult is the final molt of the female crab. During this process she is "cradled" by the jimmy crab, who forms a protective cage around her with his legs. The two crabs remain this way for several days. Immediately after the molt, mating takes place, but the jimmy continues to protect the female until her new shell has hardened. During this time, the crabs are called "doublers."

William Warner's wonderful book, *Beautiful Swimmers,* is the definitive piece of writing about blue crabs, and an absorbing and strangely moving one. Not only does Warner lead you into the many mysteries surrounding this pugnacious creature, he also paints a colorful picture of the Chesapeake Bay. His depiction of the individualism of the watermen and their speech is particularly sympathetic and fascinating.

"Oh my blessed!" an old waterman will say, "That old crab is hard to figure out."

Hard to figure out, maybe, but not at all hard to eat.

Alice Gundry's Hot Crab Canape Pie

Serves 6 to 8

1 pound crab meat

2 tablespoons capers, drained

1 teaspoon lemon juice

Dash Tabasco

1 cup mayonnaise

1 cup grated sharp cheese

Combine all ingredients except cheese. Put in buttered 10-inch pie pan. Cover with the cheese. Bake at 350° for 25 minutes or until bubbling. Serve hot with crackers.

Crab and Green Onion Pie

Serves 6

1 baked pastry shell

1½ cups grated Swiss or Gruyere cheese

2 tablespoons butter or margarine

6 green onions

½ pound crab meat

4 eggs

1 cup light cream

2 tablespoons lemon juice

½ teaspoon grated lemon peel

¼ teaspoon salt

¼ teaspoon dry mustard

Sprinkle the bottom of the pastry shell with half of the cheese. Chop onions. Preheat oven to 325°. In a frying pan, melt butter. Add onions and cook until soft. Gently mix with the crab and spoon evenly over the cheese in the pie shell.

In a bowl, beat the eggs with the cream, lemon juice, lemon peel, salt, and mustard. Pour over crab mixture. Sprinkle with remaining cheese. Bake for 55 to 60 minutes or until center is set and firm. Let cool 15 minutes. Serve warm. Can also be served at room temperature.

**Makes 2 to 4 dozen crab
meat balls depending on size**

1 pound crab meat

4 tablespoons butter

1 teaspoon salt

⅛ teaspoon cayenne

⅛ teaspoon mace

⅛ teaspoon nutmeg

1 teaspoon mustard

½ cup soft bread crumbs

2 egg yolks

Flour

Flake crab meat. Melt butter, add seasonings and bread crumbs. Mix in crab meat and beaten egg yolks. Put mixture in icebox to harden. Roll into small balls, dredge with flour and fry in deep boiling fat to a nice brown. Use to garnish fish dishes or as appetizers.

Recipe from *Maryland's Way*.

Delmarva Crab Cakes

Serves 4

1 pound crab meat

Salt and pepper

1 egg

1 stick melted butter or margarine

1 cup or less bread crumbs

1 tablespoon mayonnaise

Mix all ingredients together lightly. Make into cakes. Fry gently in pan brushed with butter or margarine. Some crab cake recipes call for seasonings such as Worcestershire or mustard. This recipe is particularly good because there is nothing to interfere with the sweet taste of the crab.

Serves 6 to 8

1	pound crab meat
6	eggs, hardboiled
½	teaspoon salt
	Dash of pepper
1	tablespoon vinegar
	Pinch of dry mustard
1	teaspoon olive oil
1	tablespoon butter
1	tablespoon flour
1	cup cream
1	four-ounce can of mushrooms, drained

Pick over crab meat and place in a large bowl. Hard boil eggs. Chop whites and add to crab meat. Add salt and pepper. Mash egg yolks. Add to them the pinch of dry mustard, the vinegar and olive oil. Mix, and add to crab meat.

Melt butter in saucepan over low heat. Blend in rounded tablespoon of flour. Add cream all at once. Cook quickly, stirring constantly until mixture thickens. Pour while hot over crab mixture. Stir together, mixing well. Add mushrooms.

Place in a buttered casserole or in ramekins. Cover tops with dots of butter and sprinkle lightly with paprika. Bake at 350° about 30 minutes, or until thoroughly heated.

From *What's Cooking In Lewes* by Elaine Mitchell. As Elaine said at the end of this recipe, this dish very deservedly won top honors for Pam Knopp of Lewes in the 1975 4-H Reddy Food Contest, when Pam was only 13 years old. Since then, Pam hasn't entered any more cooking contests. Her interests have switched to Communications—her major subject at Shippensburg University in Pennsylvania where she is a junior.

Maryland Cream of Crab Soup

Serves 6

- 1 pound crab meat
- 1 vegetable bouillon cube
- 1 cup boiling water
- ¼ cup chopped onion
- ¼ cup margarine or butter
- 2 tablespoons flour
- 1 teaspoon salt
- ¼ teaspoon celery salt
- ⅛ teaspoon pepper
  Few drops hot sauce (optional)
- 1 quart milk
  Parsley flakes or finely chopped fresh parsley for garnish

Remove cartilage from crab meat. Dissolve bouillon cube in the boiling water. In a 4-quart saucepan, cook onion in margarine or butter until tender. Blend in flour and seasonings. Add milk and bouillon gradually and cook over medium heat, stirring constantly, until mixture thickens enough to coat spoon. Add crab meat; heat, but do not boil. Garnish with parsley before serving. Serve with a hot bread and a salad for an elegant lunch.

Recipe from *An Eastern Shore Sampler* prepared by Delmarva Poultry Industry, Inc.

Teddy Kane's Carvil Hall Crab Soufflé

Serves 16

12 slices of bread, diced and crusted

7 hardboiled eggs, chopped

2½ cups mayonnaise

2½ cups milk or light cream

Buttered bread crumbs

Salt and pepper to taste

⅓ to ½ cup sherry or Vermouth

2 teaspoons dry mustard

2 pounds crab meat

Chopped parsley

Mix together all ingredients except parsley. Refrigerate overnight. Before cooking, remove from refrigerator and let stand in room temperature for 1 hour. Cover top with buttered bread crumbs. Bake in preheated 350° oven for 30 minutes or until bubbly and golden brown. Decorate each serving with parsley.

Chapter 7

DELMARVALOUS ARSTERS, ARSTERMEN, CLAMS, AND CLAMMERS

Love life among the "arsters" is more interesting than you might think. Oysters can change their sex whenever they want. It seems less energy is involved in being a male oyster than in being a female one. (So what else is new?) So when the going gets rough, male oysters abound.

Young oysters on Delmarva (*Crassostrea virginica*) are predominantly male, but toward the end of their first year many change into females. Who decides who will become which is a question not answered by the authorities. Oysters' hearts beat faster when their shells are open than when the shells are closed. What's more, oysters have TWO hearts, the accessory one agitating the blood in the mantle.

Having two hearts doesn't increase romance among *Crassostrea*, though, for the whole operation of producing eggs and fertilizing them takes place within one oyster.

This dismal practice has not lessened in any way man's appetite for these bivalves. Long before the Christian era, the Chinese and the Romans practiced oyster farming in order to satisfy the tastes of their epicures. Many Roman houses had tanks of water containing oysters for eating.

On Delmarva, oyster feasting has been popular for at least 10,000 years. The Indians left great piles of shells (middens) all over the Peninsula. When the Europeans first arrived, oysters were so plentiful that ships often ran aground on huge oyster reefs. Not true any more, alas.

An oyster can live to be 100 years old—if it's not pestered, that is. Oyster pesterers abound. Oyster drills, or borers, drill through oyster shells, then eat the meat with long tongues. Pea crabs are little enough to crawl between the shells. Starfish pry the shells apart. Some fish, such as black drums, have "teeth" that can crush oysters. And then there's man, the greatest predator of them all.

Pollution and over-fishing have affected oyster abundance. Natural disasters such as hurricanes and extremely cold winters take their toll. In the late 1800s, 15 million bushels of oysters were caught annually in Maryland waters. In the 1980–81 season, September to March 31st, 2,450,661 bushels were gathered, and the fact is that each year we are now harvesting more oysters than are produced.

"Arstermen" have invented lots of ways to get at these salty morsels; all of the methods require physical stamina. Some oystermen go after the bivalves by hand, wearing hip boots and slogging around in cold water all day. Others set forth in boats to tong the oysters by hand or with mechanical tongs or by dredging. A recent method is to scuba dive for them, a practice which has old-time watermen up in arms. Watermen even tong for oysters when the waters are frozen. Chunks of ice are cut away and the tongers reach through the holes to grab their prey.

Oyster tongs were developed in the 17th century. Hand tongs are like scissors with rakes at the ends, and it requires great strength and endurance to operate them. In the late 19th century, sailing dredge boats were developed. Today, both sailing and motorized workboats are used. For all methods used, there are strict regulations governing the how's, where's, and when's of "arsterin."

To encourage young oysters—spats—and oyster growth, a cultch of old oyster shells can be implanted on the existing beds. This is done when the weather is fine and the state has enough money. On the cultch, seed oysters are spread. In the summer of 1982, 288,000 bushels of seed oysters were planted in Maryland's waters, but mature oysters still don't number enough to keep up with demand.

Ever since anyone can remember, there have been fierce struggles over oyster harvesting. Oyster wars between Maryland and Virginia watermen have been and still are violent, full-scale combats. Who can go "arsterin" where is the issue. A sizeable number of watermen have been shot, killed, or wounded for oystering in the wrong waters.

Gunfire wounded two Maryland watermen during the 1982 season, and the fighting will probably continue. The mother of one of the wounded men, a Crisfield, Maryland, woman, was quoted as saying the fighting will never cease. "Not as long as there's oysters out there," she said.

So fierce and hard-fought have the oyster wars been that an engrossing book has been written about them. *The Oyster Wars of Chesapeake Bay*, by John Wennersten, reads like a dime-store thriller. It contains tales of men being shanghaied to work on oyster boats, of oyster poachers, of oyster pirates, and of an oyster police patrol—all laced liberally with gunfire, bloodshed, and violence. Chapters such as "Hell on the Half Shell" may cause you to look at your next fried oyster with new respect. "Arsterin" is no occupation for a pantywaist.

Chesapeake oystermen are on the verge of becoming an extinct species, Wennersten believes. Pollution and over-fishing are taking their toll. And it is harder and harder for men to earn a decent living by oystering, in spite of the long hours oystermen devote to their backbreaking work.

"While there will always be oysters," Wennersten writes, "there soon won't be watermen to hunt them. The oystermen of the Bay country are being overwhelmed by the problems of an urban technological society, and their passing will scarcely be noticed."

That will be a sad day for Delmarva.

Delmarva's clams are not as famous as its oysters. There is an abundance of them, though, and lots of people, residents and vacationers alike, enjoy arming themselves with clam rakes and "goin' clammin."

Maybe you think a clam is a clam is a clam and so what? Nevertheless, distinctions should be made, for there are about 15,000 species of bivalves, or two-shelled mollusks, that fall under the general heading of clams (including "arsters"). The word clam, incidentally, refers to the tightness with which a bivalve's shell closes. The term comes from an Anglo-Saxon word, "klemm," meaning to grasp or clamp.

A very ancient form of life, clams have been around since Paleozoic times, 500,000,000 years ago. This makes them hundreds of millions of years older than man, give or take a millenium or two. Over the years, clams have adapted to living in salt water, brackish water, or fresh water. A few even manage to survive several months out of water entirely, a happy adaptation to the fact that some ponds dry up.

Many bivalves live in the muddy bottoms of shallow bodies of water. Others make their homes in hard, rocky habitats, or even wood (shipworms). The depths at which bivalves live also vary widely. Some prefer the shallows while others have been found as deep as 17,400 feet. Clams also may vary in size from a tiny species 4/100ths of an inch wide to huge, 4-foot-wide giant clams weighing 500 pounds.

As is true of "arsters," lots of animals besides man prey on clams. Whelks (marine snails) drill holes through clam shells to feed on the animals inside. Gulls drop clams on hard surfaces to break the shells and extract the meat. Some gastropods (univalves) have convenient gizzards that can grind up the clam shell, so they consume the whole clam. Some fish eat bivalves. Crabs like them. Walruses feed on clams, and are said to dig them up with their tusks. One kind of gastropod grabs a clam by the foot (yes, clams have a foot, that's how they get around), then uses a spine to force open the clam shell. And, of course, there's man, who has dredged, dug, raked, and dived for clams. Man has eaten them, made money (wampum) from them, extracted pearls and mother of pearl from them, and even made buttons from them. He has used clam shells for cooking, for ashtrays, and for lining garden paths. Large ones make handsome bird baths. They are ground up for use on paths and driveways. When used with silver bells, clam shells make gardens grow, as in "Mary, Mary, Quite Contrary."

Some clams, such as scallops, can swim to escape all these enemies. But the only defense most clams have against predators is to burrow. That they do this well is evidenced by their having survived successfully through the long unrolling of the geological time span. When their enemies leave them alone, they can live a surprising length of time. Some, like the oyster, can become senior-citizen mollusks of 80 to 100 years old.

Clams have blood, hearts, eyes, nervous systems, sensory organs, and practically everything else man has except a head as such. Some bivalves, like oysters, can change sex at will. Others such as mussels show distinct differences between the males and females.

All of which brings us to Delmarva clams, which are quite different from West Coast clams. Out on the West Coast, butter clams, geoducks (gooey-ducks), and razor clams thrive. Here quahogs, surf clams, and soft-shell clams abound.

Quahog (*Mercenaria venus mercenaria*—a gold-digger clam?) may also be spelled quahaug or quauhog, and is a corruption of the Indian word for this clam, "paquahock." Quahogs are found all along the East Coast and in great numbers along the Delaware coast. Amateur clammers rake for them in mud just below the level of high tide or in the muddy bottoms of tidal streams. Indians made wampum out of the purple part of the quahog shell. Quahogs less than 2¼ inches long are called "littlenecks." Those up to 3 inches long are called "cherrystones." Larger ones are just plain old quahogs and are usually chopped up for chowder.

Most surf clams (*Spisula solidissima*) live on the Continental Shelf, the submerged outer edge of the East Coast. Storms may move these clams away from their customary habitat, washing them ashore in great numbers, where, at low tide, they may be gathered with the bare hands. These clams grow to 7 inches in length and are the ones people like to take home as ashtrays.

Soft-shell clams (*Mya arenaria*) were first termed maninose by Indian tribes around the Chesapeake Bay. Maninose are found all along the eastern seaboard, though they are called such only on Delmarva. Usually they are obtained commercially by dredging. Amateurs go after them with forks. Maninose have very long necks that make convenient handles when humans steam them and dip them in melted butter.

There are dozens of ways to eat any of these Delmarva bivalves, from raw to Oysters Rockefeller. A few suggestions follow.

On Puget Sound, in Washington State, where I grew up, we used to get our clams ready for eating by first scrubbing them hard with a brush. Then we put them in a big dish pan and covered them with salt water, or with fresh water to which salt had been added. We strewed cornmeal on top of the water and left the clams in a cool place overnight. The clams would open up, eat the corn meal, and get rid of any sand in their stomachs, doing this in a manner known only to clams and marine biologists. I still use this method.

Clam or Oyster Fritters

Serves 4 to 6

1 pint oysters or clams

2 eggs

½ cup milk for oyster fritters

½ cup clam juice for clam fritters

2 cups flour

2 teaspoons baking powder

½ teaspoon salt

⅛ teaspoon pepper

If the oysters or clams are small, leave them whole. Otherwise, chop them into small bits. Make a batter of the eggs, milk or clam juice, flour, baking powder, salt, and pepper. Stir the clams or oysters into the batter and drop by spoonfuls into deep hot fat (360° to 370°). Fry until golden brown. The fritters may also be sautéed in butter.

Oyster Loaf 79

Serves 6

- 1 pint oysters, standards, fresh or frozen
- ½ teaspoon salt
- ⅛ teaspoon pepper
- 2 eggs, beaten
- ¼ cup milk
- ¾ cup flour
- 2 cups soft bread crumbs
- ½ cup melted margarine or butter
- 2 loaves French bread
  Fat for deep frying
- ½ cup Tartar sauce
- 1½ cups shredded lettuce
- 18 thin tomato slices

Drain oysters and dry between absorbent paper. Sprinkle with salt and pepper. Combine eggs and milk. Roll oysters in flour, dip into egg mixture, then roll in bread crumbs to coat evenly. Refrigerate at least 30 minutes. Slice bread loaves in half horizontally. Scoop out inside of loaf, leaving about ¾ inch of bread all the way around. Brush the bread shells with melted margarine. Place bread shells on baking sheet and bake in moderate oven, 350°, 3 to 5 minutes until warm and crisp. Place oysters in a single layer in a fry basket. Fry in deep fat, 350° for 2 to 3 minutes. Drain on absorbent paper. Spread inside of bread shells with tartar sauce. Place shredded lettuce in the bottom halves of the loaves. Arrange tomato slices on lettuce and fried oysters on top of the tomatoes. Cover with top halves of the loaves of bread. Cut each loaf into 3 portions.

From Robert Robinson's *Shellfish Heritage Cookbook, Part 1.*

Note: Try adding herbs to the melted margarine: 3 tablespoons sesame seeds, 1 tablespoon dried thyme, and 1 teaspoon poultry seasoning. A dash of garlic powder adds zest. Chopped chives are good, too. Also try substituting mayonnaise for the tartar sauce, and sprinkling a little lemon juice over the cooked oysters.

Allow ¾ to 1 quart clams
per person

Put well-scrubbed and purified steamer clams (see Puget Sound Clam Purification) in a large pan with very little water. One-half to 1 cup is plenty as the clams will eject liquid as they are cooking. Cover. Cook with the lid slightly ajar until the clams are open, about 10 to 15 minutes. Serve on flat soup plates with melted butter on the side.

Some people like to add onion and garlic to the butter. Other sauces may be used—Tartar sauce, mayonnaise, tomato—but melted butter is the favorite accompaniment. The same rule that applies to all Delmarvalous foods applies to clams as well: when you have a wonderfully flavored natural product, there is no need to doll it up.

The clam broth is good to drink, either straight or mixed with tomato juice. A jigger of vodka adds zest for some.

Chapter 8

HOOK, LINE, AND SINKER

With more water than Noah ever dreamed of, Delmarva naturally has a lot of fin fish and fishermen. Teeming in Peninsula waters at various times of the year are sea trout, flounder, bluefish, tarpon, bass, cod, shad, croaker, mackerel, herring, tautog, cunner, pollock, blowfish, black drum, smelt, and alewives, to name just a FEW.

Humans pursue these silvery swimmers in a variety of ways. All kinds of commercial fishing ventures exist, and the arguments between the commercial fishermen and the sports fishermen are constant, each side accusing the other of ruining the fishing.

Commercial fishing methods vary according to the type of fish being sought. The chief methods used are trawling, seining, gill netting, and line fishing. All of these practices are made increasingly deadly with the use of more and more sophisticated devices—electronic instruments and helicopters to spot the schools of fish, machinery to haul in the nets and lines, tough and incredibly durable man-made fibres, fast diesel ships to follow the schools of fish, electronically aimed and thrown spears for large fish, and huge factory ships that process the fish. Men who make a living on the sea always brave dangers from the elements, but the contest between fish and man in commercial fishing is no longer an even battle.

The sports fishermen may surf cast, troll, deep-sea fish (take along your Dramamine), fly cast in rivers, or drop a hook, line, and worm from a bridge or dock. Some docks and jetties provide fishermen with such abundant catches that vacationers come from distant states just to dip their lines in Delmarva waters.

When warm weather arrives in this watery area, fishermen can be seen everywhere you look—on bridges, jetties, and docks, along streams and shorelines, in rowboats near land, in power boats heading out to deeper waters. All of them are seeking that moment of thrill when the line jerks, and the contest between man and fish begins.

Over the years, I have come to treasure all life, and can no longer kill anything for fun or sport. But watching the hopeful eagerness of children as they drop their lines into the water from the bridge near our house brings back memories of earlier fishing days.

A wonderful black woman, Cassie Mae Childress, was an indispensable part of our family when our daughter, Catherine, was growing up. It was she who taught Cath to fish. I can see them now, Cassie Mae in a print dress and apron, sitting on the dock with her back against the post and her legs stretched out in front of her. Slowly, slowly, Cassie Mae would pull the fishing pole back and forth, hoping to lure the fish. The child, wearing blonde braids, shorts, and an air of total concentration, would be seated on the dock with her legs dangling over the edge, or standing in a rowboat moored nearby. In her hands would be a long, slightly flexible branch onto which had been tied a line, a red-and-white bobber or cork, a small sinker, and a hook with a worm on it. The two shared a coffee can filled with damp earth and freshly dug angleworms. If someone in the family had driven into Chestertown recently, he might have stopped at the tree-shaded general store where a battered sign proclaimed that they carried "BEER AND BLOODWORMS." In that event, there could also be on the dock a small cardboard ice cream carton with a wire handle that would be filled with damp moss and bloodworms.

"Ssshh! SSSHH!" Cassie Mae would whisper. "You hush and be still Catherine Marvin, or you scare dem fish. Jes you sit dere, honey, and don' you move a eyelash. Don' you even swat a skeeter. If'n you gotta say sumpin', you wisper. An alla tahm, you talk to dat dere fish down dere wiff yore heart. Prit soon, you'll see dat silver fishy movin', movin', nosin' roun' yore line. Den he'll take a lil nibble of dat juicy worm, and dat's wen you'll have 'im. Dat's wen we'll git us dat priddy silver fishy for our supper."

It worked, too. Obviously Cassie Mae exuded some kind of magnetism that traveled from her to the swimmers in the clear, cool waters of Maryland's Fairlee Creek, pulling the fish irresistibly toward their ultimate fate at the end of Cassie Mae's line. Many are the wonderful meals we have had of freshly caught rockfish fried in corn-meal, with a side dish of Cassie Mae's "messa Creecy greens."

May your fishing be as magical when you visit Delmarva. Even without a visit, may your fish entrées from any of the following suggestions be as tasty as Cassie Mae's fried rockfish.

Bouillabaisse, Old-Fashioned Delmarva Way

Serves 6 to 8

½ cup olive oil

1 large onion, sliced

1 or 2 leeks, sliced

2 cloves garlic, minced

1 bay leaf

2 cups chopped peeled tomatoes

2 cups fish stock or 1 cup water and 1 cup clam juice

1 cup dry white wine

¼ cup chopped fresh fennel or ½ teaspoon crushed fennel seed

⅛ teaspoon crushed saffron

1 teaspoon salt

¼ teaspoon pepper

2 tablespoons minced parsley

2 lobster tails, shell sliced open

1 pound red snapper

1 pound halibut

12 shrimp

6 large crab legs

6 mussels (optional)

6 clams

6 oysters

Heat oil in large pot. Add onion, leek, garlic, bay leaf, and cook until onion is tender. Add tomatoes, stock, wine, saffron, fennel, salt, pepper, and parsley. Simmer 15 minutes. Add lobster (in shell), snapper, and halibut that have been cut into chunks, and cook 10 minutes. Rinse shrimp and crab and scrub clams, oysters, and mussels. Add shell fish and cook 5 minutes or until shells open. Ladle into large soup plates and serve with crusty bread.

Recipe from *The Last Resort Cookbook*.

Serves 6 to 8

1 bottle clam juice

1 package frozen fish (any kind)

1 can clams and juice

2 cans stewed tomatoes

1 can or package crab meat

1 large onion, chopped

1 large green pepper, chopped

6 strips bacon cut in pieces

1 teaspoon garlic powder

In a heavy soup pan cook the bacon until just done. Add chopped onion and chopped pepper. Cook gently until onion clears. Add rest of ingredients. Simmer 10 minutes. Serve over toast placed in individual bowls.

Cape May Goodies

"During the last two weeks in August, a small fish appears in the Delaware Bay sometimes erroneously called a croaker. But it is smaller than a croaker and is called a 'spot' or a 'Cape May Goody.' It is a very sweet and delicious fish.

"Herbert Orton said that his father used to put a layer of rock salt in a container, cover this with a layer of the fish, another of salt, another layer of fish, and so on. He would add water to cover. In the winter, he would take out a fish each morning, boil it, and have it for breakfast. This was a common practice among people living near the Delaware Bay."

The above note on "goodies" is by Ruth Chambers Stewart, Lewes, Delaware.

Note: These "goodies" also lend themselves well to being dipped in corn meal and gently fried in butter or margarine until golden brown on each side. See recipe for Fried Herring, Smelt, or Other Small Fish.

How to Bake Shad to Dissolve the Bones

**Five or 6 pounds of shad
serves 4 people**

Shad

2 or 3 tablespoons butter

Salt to taste

Juice of 1½ lemons

Put the shad on a large sheet of heavy aluminum foil. Dot with butter. Add salt and lemon juice. Fold the foil over the fish, and crimp edges tightly. Place on a shallow pan. Bake for 6 to 8 hours at 250°. The bones will dissolve, and the fish will be juicy and tender.

Chesapeake Bay Shad Roe

Serves 4

4 sets shad roe

3 tablespoons butter

6 to 8 shallots, minced

8 to 10 medium-sized mushrooms, wiped clean and sliced, or 1 small can sliced mushrooms

4 tablespoons minced parsley

½ cup dry white wine

1 cup heavy cream

1 tablespoon flour

Melt butter in a large skillet, stir in shallots and parsley. Cook slowly 1 minute. Stir in mushrooms and cook 5 minutes, shaking pan frequently. Carefully add shad roe, cover with wine and simmer, covered, 15 minutes. Let steam escape occasionally. Put cream and flour in a jar and shake until free of lumps. Remove roe from pan, reduce liquid to half, stir in cream mixture and cook until slightly thickened. Put roe on a flame-proof platter. Pour sauce over it and broil 3 minutes.

Recipe from *Heartland*.

Shad roe sets (Allow 1 set per person if sets are small. If sets are large, half a set will serve one person.)
Boiling water
1 teaspoon salt
1 tablespoon vinegar
Pepper to taste
Butter or margarine
Sliced lemon
Chopped parsley

Separate shad roe sets if large. If small, leave together. Handle the sets carefully. To avoid breakage, cook only 1 set at a time. Place in a shallow pan and cover with boiling water. Add salt and vinegar. Cook over a very low heat until white and firm.

Drain and cover with cold water. Re-drain, and put aside until ready to use.

Season roe with salt and pepper, and sauté in butter or margarine (butter burns more quickly), cooking the roe very slowly so eggs won't explode. Turn only once. When brown on both sides, remove to plate and add lemon and parsley.

Delicious served with bacon and hot grits or spoon bread.

Fried Herring, Smelt, or Other Small Fish

Roll slightly damp fish in cornmeal, salt, and pepper. Fry gently in margarine until brown on both sides. Serve with a green salad, warm French bread, and sweet butter . . . a meal fit for Delmarva kings in the dappled light of a summer day.

Striped Bass (Rockfish) Stuffed with Crab Meat

Serves 4 to 6

1 striped bass 3 to 5 pounds
Salt
Pepper
2 tablespoons chopped onion
¼ cup chopped celery
½ cup butter
2 cups soft bread crumbs
1 cup flaked crab meat
1 tablespoon chopped parsley
1 cup milk
1 large onion, sliced
Parsley
Lemon

Wash the bass and sprinkle it inside and out with salt and pepper. Sauté chopped onion and celery in ¼ cup of butter until lightly browned. Mix together the sautéed vegetables, bread crumbs, crab meat, chopped parsley, salt and pepper. Stuff fish and secure with skewers, or sew it together. Place fish in a shallow baking dish, and put milk and sliced onion in the pan. Pour ¼ cup melted butter over fish. Bake uncovered in a moderate oven (350°) for about 45 minutes. Garnish top of fish with thin slices of lemon dipped in chopped parsley.

Recipe from *Maryland's Way*.

Mary Holt Grey's Fish Chowder

is a superlative chowder featuring the unique use of fried salt pork cubes as croutons. Served from a tureen and accompanied by a salad and hot bread, it makes a wonderful focus for a small winter luncheon such as a Christmas tree decorating party. When we used it thus one year, one of the guests turned to his wife and said, "Woman! Why don't you ever serve good hearty soup like this?"

Mary Holt Grey is a Maine Downeaster who was transplanted south by marrying a Virginian. Such a switch might imply some kind of culture shock. Interestingly enough, in spite of climatic differences, New Englanders and Southerners are much alike, particularly in good manners, graciousness, and the ability to create a pleasant life style.

You may make the chowder with either fresh or frozen fish. It is best to thaw frozen fish before starting the chowder. The original recipe called for haddock, but any skinless, white-fleshed fish will do.

Serves 4

1 pound of fish
2 medium potatoes, peeled and thinly sliced
2 medium onions, thinly sliced
Salt and pepper
1 small can condensed milk and enough fresh milk to make 3 cups in all
2 tablespoons butter
1½ cups water

Melt butter in soup kettle, add onions, and cook but do not brown. Then add potatoes and the water. Boil until potatoes are almost cooked. Add the fish, which will take 6 to 10 minutes to cook. Add milk, salt and pepper.

Before serving, cut ¾ pound of salt pork into ¼-inch squares and cook slowly in a frying pan until brown and crisp. These brown best if you keep pouring off the fat.

Sprinkle salt pork cubes on top of the soup.

Chapter 9

DELMARVA'S GOLDEN EGG—THE BROILER-FRYER

Just 50 years ago, the campaign promise for a presidential election was "A chicken in every pot." Back then, chicken for Sunday dinner was a special treat, as it had been for at least 400 years. As Page Smith and Charles Daniel pointed out in *The Chicken Book*, Henry IV had promised the same thing in the 16th century. "If God grants me the usual length of life, I hope to make France so prosperous that every peasant will have a chicken in his pot on Sunday," said Henry.

Now, thanks to modern methods of producing and marketing poultry, chicken is everyday fare. What's more, today's chickens are undoubtedly a lot plumper and tastier than the scrawny fowl served back in Henry's time.

Delmarvans, particularly, should count their blessings. The poultry business on the Peninsula has become the fourth largest in the country. Arkansas is first. Then come Georgia, Alabama, and Delmarva.

In 1981, 433 million chickens were processed on Delmarva. Over 18,000 people were employed in the industry, and the final value of the birds was $775 million. And these figures keep growing.

The annual Poultry Festival celebrates all this prosperity. The Delmarva Poultry Industry, Inc., an organization with 4,000 members, works for the continued progress of poultry farming and processing.

Because the poultry industry is the backbone of the local economy, the Poultry Festival is an important annual event on the Peninsula. For over 30 years the festival has been held in various locations around Delmarva. Changes in the festival's make-up have reflected the growing popularity of chicken as a food and the expanding role of Delmarva in the huge national market.

The first festival, held in Georgetown, Delaware, in 1948, was sponsored by the University of Delaware Agricultural Sub-station there.

To add breadth to the occasion the A. & P. (The Great Atlantic & Pacific Tea Company) sponsored a nationwide competition to develop a broad-breasted, meatier chicken. People, particularly geneticists, came from all over the country. They contributed ideas for developing tender, young chickens. Consumers wanted better chickens than the then frequently offered birds of doubtful age that required recipes like "Supreme of Old Hen."

In that first year, the Delaware hosts for this national contest staged a festive pageant to welcome participants from other states. The next year, everybody concerned thought even a little more pizzazz could be achieved by having a chicken-cooking contest. That first cook-off, sponsored by the Delmarva Poultry Industry, included finalists from Delaware, Maryland, Virginia, and Washington, D.C. The contest kept growing and changing until 1971. By then the contest had become such a large promotional event that many felt that national sponsorship was called for. The National Broiler Council, headquartered in Washington, D.C., became the new backer. It is interesting to note that the brain child of a small group of Delmarva poultry industry supporters had become one of the largest and most successful food promotions in the country.

The first festival under national sponsorship was held in 1972. For 10 years thereafter, preliminary regional chicken cook-offs were held, with winners going on to compete in the national contest. On Delmarva there were three winners annually, one from each of the Peninsula states—Delaware, Maryland, and Virginia. These three won $500 each, plus transportation to the national contest, plus various appliances and household goods. National cook-offs were held in states such as Georgia, South Carolina, Florida, and Maryland. First-prize winners pocketed $10,000, along with an addition $10,000 worth of lesser prizes, which is no chicken feed.

In 1983, the chicken cooking contest took yet another turn. The national contest moved to an alternate-year plan, with regional contests, such as the Delmarva Chicken Cooking Contest, being held in the off years. But the Peninsula event expanded to include all the northeastern states where Delmarva chicken is marketed—Maine, New Hampshire, Vermont, Massachusetts, Connecticut, Rhode Island, New York, New Jersey, Pennsylvania, Delaware, Maryland, Virginia, and Washington, D.C. Rain, snow, or shine, every night 150 refrigerator trucks loaded with poultry leave Delmarva, arriving early the following morning at markets all over the northeast. Delmarva's location within a few hours of major metropolitan markets allows speedy delivery to northeastern consumers.

Fowls were the earliest animals to be domesticated. People in China raised poultry as early as 1400 B.C. Both the Chinese and Egyptians developed incubators that could hatch up to 10,000 chickens. Undoubtedly, mass production of food was developed to feed the vast number of people working on the pyramids in Egypt and on the Great Wall of China.

But chickens have played other roles as well. They have been worshiped by various cultures. The Greeks, Egyptians, and Romans all sacrificed cocks in religious rites. Many cultures have associated cocks with miracles.

Chickens have been used in divination, magic, and prophecy. In fact, in Ceylon, the Vedda are reluctant to eat chickens because chickens are considered sacred birds. Tibetan lamas won't eat chickens or eggs for much the same reason. As *The Chicken Book* points out, in much of the Arabian world, eggs are looked down on by the well-to-do as food for the poor. In Saudi Arabia, some people do keep chickens for religious or magical purposes, but never eat the flesh or eggs. In the Middle Ages, people thought that if you found an egg with two yolks, your wish would be granted. Think of all the wishes that would come true nowadays by eating those extra large brown eggs, almost all of which have two yolks.

The use of chickens in the "sport" of cockfighting cannot be overlooked. The origins of cockfighting have been lost in the mists of antiquity, but it is certainly true that this is a universal sport that has been practiced for thousands of years.

It is odd that such a useful and so often revered bird as the chicken has given its name to so many derogatory phrases. True, a "spring chicken" and a "chick" are complimentary. But what about "old hen," "hen party," and "hen-pecked?" An arrogant man is "cock-sure," a less fortunate one is "cock-eyed." You're "chicken" if you are cowardly, though no one seems to know why the word is used thus. And, of course, there is the "cocktail," another word of mysterious origin. And certainly an "egghead" has come to be a term of derision.

The late 1700s and early 1800s have been called the Century of the Chicken. When some Cochin fowls were presented to the young Queen Victoria, they were a sensation. From then on, every gentleman farmer took to breeding chickens to obtain a rarer, handsomer, more vari-colored chicken with dazzling plumage. Poultry mania swept over the world. The results were spectacular: the mammoth Brahma weighing 12 pounds; the tiny Bantam weighing 20 ounces; the brilliantly spangled Hamburg, or the sombre Orpington; the long-tailed Yokohama, or the cushion-tailed Cochin. Plumage varies greatly both in color and form—the spangled, laced, pencilled, striped, barred, the solid-colored. There are birds with ragged feathers, frizzled feathers, downy, and silky feathers. You may see leaf combs, pea combs, bearded birds, feather-shanked birds . . . and, and, and. These chickens live in elegance, and in their heyday occupied houses often costing as much as a small cottage.

Alas, for chickens, someone decided that the chicken must earn not only its own keep, but also that of its master. Therein started the industrialization of the chicken, and its decline.

Delmarva concentrates on chickens whether they are in decline or upswing. And just to twist your mind a little, think on this: Samuel Butler said that a hen is only an egg's way of making another egg. And don't forget that no matter how clever you are, you can never unscramble an egg.

You have to stay with this. You can't go away for very long.

Serves 3 to 4 people, depending on appetites

1 chicken, cut in pieces (or packages of chicken pieces)
Crisco
Flour
Salt and pepper to taste
1 cup milk

For 1 good-sized chicken (2½ to 3 pounds) you will need 2 large frying pans. (Cast iron frying pans are best.) Melt enough Crisco to get ¼ inch or so in each pan. Shake chicken pieces in a <u>heavy</u> brown paper bag containing the flour, salt, and pepper. You'll probably have to add more flour, salt, and pepper as you go along. Put chicken into heated oil and cook <u>very slowly</u>, turning as necessary. Remove such quick-cooking pieces as livers, hearts, and necks to a platter warming on the stove. Make sure chicken is <u>done</u>, not still red around the bones. Test it with a fork. The flesh should separate easily. When all pieces are done, remove to the platter, and make gravy. ("You mean you make <u>milk</u> gravy?" a horrified Italian friend asked. Of course you make milk gravy! Otherwise, it wouldn't be Delmarvalous fried chicken.)

Gravy: Some cooks approach gravies and sauces apprehensively. The secret of avoiding sauce or gravy disasters lies in using a <u>thin</u> roux (the mixture of flour and butter, margarine, grease, or other fat). Before adding liquid, the roux should be no thicker than heavy cream. Thicker roux tends to produce gravy with lumps unless great care is taken in adding liquid very slowly. Proportions of 2 tablespoons of melted fat to 1 rounded tablespoon of flour and 1 cup of milk will result in a satiny smooth gravy or sauce.

For your chicken gravy, therefore, after you have removed the cooked chicken from the pan, combine cooking oil and cooked crumbs from both pans into one. Pour off excess grease, leaving approximately 2 tablespoons in the pan. Place pan over medium-high heat. Add 1 rounded tablespoon of flour. Stir until smooth. Add 1 cup of milk all at once, stirring constantly until mixture is thickened. Voila! A gourmet gravy.

This will make about 1 cup of gravy. If you want twice that, double the amounts of each ingredient.

Almost always, when frying a whole chicken, cooks do double the amount of gravy, including the giblets, which are considered special delicacies. Giblet gravy, when the giblets are cooked separately in water or broth with onions and herbs, is usually confined to turkey and involves an entirely different process.

Serve with fluffy mashed potatoes, a green vegetable, easy rave-producing biscuits, and honey. On a hot summer day, substitute potato salad and sliced tomatoes for the mashed potatoes, gravy, and biscuits. None of the above is at all thinning, but Oh! My Dear! Is it ever Delmarvadelicious.

Perdue's Parsleyed Egg Noodles with Giblets

Delmarva's Perdue chickens are fat, golden, and juicy. They have become justly famous on their own merits. They have also been brilliantly promoted by Frank Perdue on TV and by recipe tags on the chickens themselves. When it comes to chicken giblets, Frank Perdue delivers a little lecture to potential cooks. "It has come to my attention," he writes on a giblet wrapper, "that as good as my giblets are, some people are throwing them away. They don't know what to do with them.

"Now it seems to me, after all the trouble I take to make sure a Perdue chicken's as good inside as it is outside, you should have a chance to eat the whole thing. Not waste any part of it.

"So I'm giving you one of my recipes. That way I make sure my giblets end up in the right place."

Serves 4 to 6

Giblets and necks from 2 chickens

6 tablespoons butter

1 medium onion, chopped

8 ounces medium egg noodles

1 tablespoon salt

½ cup heavy cream

½ teaspoon tarragon

½ teaspoon thyme

3 tablespoons fresh, chopped parsley

Freshly ground pepper

Cook giblets and necks in simmering water for 25 minutes. Meanwhile, heat 2 tablespoons butter in skillet, and sauté onions for 3 minutes. Set aside. In large pot, bring 3½ cups water to a boil and add 1 tablespoon salt. Add noodles and cook until just tender, about 7 minutes. Meanwhile, drain giblets and necks. Chop the meat. Drain noodles. Toss with remaining 4 tablespoons of butter and heavy cream. Add giblets, onions, and herbs. Season to taste with salt and pepper.

Serves 3 to 4

6 to 8 pieces of chicken

2 lemons

½ cup flour

1 teaspoon salt

½ teaspoon pepper

½ cup salad oil

½ teaspoon paprika

2 tablespoons brown sugar

1 cup chicken broth (may be made with bouillon cubes)

Wash and drain the chicken. Grate the lemon peel of one lemon and set aside. Cut lemon in half, and squeeze juice over the pieces of chicken, rubbing each piece well with the juice. Shake chicken in a paper bag with the flour, salt, pepper, and paprika. Brown slowly in the salad oil. Arrange in a casserole. Sprinkle the grated lemon peel over the chicken. Sprinkle the brown sugar over the top. Cover with the thinly sliced second lemon. Pour over this the chicken broth. Cover with aluminum foil. Bake in a preheated 375° oven 40 to 45 minutes, or until fork tender.

Stewed Chicken with Dumplings

Serves 4 to 6

1 large stewing chicken

Celery tops

1 onion, chopped

1 teaspoon salt

½ teaspoon pepper

3 tablespoons flour

3 tablespoons butter

Pinch of powdered thyme

1 bay leaf

Cut chicken in serving pieces and place in heavy stewing pan. Barely cover with water. Add celery tops, onion, bay leaf, thyme, salt, and pepper. Bring to a boil slowly. Reduce heat. Cover and simmer until tender. Remove chicken and keep it hot. Strain broth, return to stew pot and thicken with flour mixed with softened butter. Bring to a boil. When bubbling, add dumplings.

Light Dumplings

1 cup flour
½ teaspoon salt
1 teaspoon baking powder
Pinch of baking soda
1 tablespoon melted butter
⅜ to ½ cup milk (sufficient to make a soft dough)

Combine ingredients and drop by spoonfuls into the hot liquid. Cover tightly. Boil for 20 minutes exactly without lifting lid. Serve at once with chicken and gravy.

Recipe from *Maryland's Way*.

Slippery Dumplings

Slippery dumplings are imported from Pennsylvania. They are like flat noodles. Fans adore them. In a chicken and dumpling recipe, they may be substituted for raised dumplings.

Serves 4

3 cups flour
6 tablespoons shortening, slightly rounded
3 teaspoons salt
About 1 cup of warm water

Place the flour and salt in a large mixing bowl; add the shortening and cut in with pastry blender until blended. Add the warm water a little at a time. You may need more water, or a little less.

Roll out approximately ⅛-inch thick. Cut dumplings into squares approximately 1½ inches by 2 inches. As you cut them, place on a floured plate, flouring lightly between layers. Put in refrigerator until ready to cook. Bring chicken broth to a boil. Add dumplings, one at a time, stirring gently and occasionally to keep dumplings separated. When all dumplings are in, turn heat down to slow boil and cook 15 to 20 minutes. You may leave them covered or uncovered.

Recipe from *What's Cooking in Lewes* by Elaine Mitchell.

Townsend's, Inc., in Millsboro, Delaware, is a huge processor of chickens. Many of their fans think Townsend's produces the best chickens in the world, and will drive miles to buy them. They are available in some local markets, but most Townsend chickens are shipped out of state.

All the Townsends are good cooks. Here are two of their favorite recipes.

Meredith's Easy Chicken Dinner

Serves 4 to 6

1	can celery soup
1	can cream of chicken soup
1	soup-can-full dry Vermouth
1	big onion chopped
1	package Uncle Ben's wild and long grain rice
8 to 10	small chicken breasts
1	package Lipton's onion soup mix

Mix together soups, Vermouth, onion and rice. Spread mixture in a shallow, buttered casserole. Top with chicken. Sprinkle onion soup mix over chicken. Cover and refrigerate overnight. Next day, bake at 350° for 1 hour covered, then 1 hour uncovered.

Coley's and Susy's Chicken in a Basket

The original of this recipe in *The California Heritage Cookbook* called for a round loaf of sourdough bread. Round loaves of sourdough bread, however, are scarcer than palm trees on Delmarva. A good variation can be made by using any oblong or round uncut loaf of bread.

Serves 3 to 4

½ cup flour

1½ tablespoons sesame seeds

½ tablespoon dried thyme

¾ tablespoon dried tarragon

½ tablespoon poppy seeds

1 teaspoon each salt and pepper

8 chicken thighs

2 egg whites, lightly beaten

2 tablespoons butter

2 tablespoons margarine

1 loaf uncut bread

Combine the flour, sesame seeds, thyme, tarragon, poppy seeds, salt and pepper. Dip the chicken thighs in the beaten egg whites, then coat each piece with the flour mixture. Melt the butter and margarine in a large skillet. Brown the chicken, about 7 minutes on each side, over medium heat. Place in a casserole, cover, and bake 40 minutes in a preheated 350° oven.

While chicken is baking, prepare the bread basket. You will need the bread and the following ingredients for a butter and herb sauce:

4 tablespoons butter

3 tablespoons sesame seeds

1 tablespoon dried thyme

1½ teaspoons dried tarragon

1 tablespoon poppy seeds

Melt the butter, and add the other ingredients. Cut a large top in the bread. Scoop out the inside, leaving about ½-inch of bread all the way around. With a pastry brush, spread the butter, seed and herb sauce over the inside of the loaf and the inside of the top. Place the loaf and top on a cookie sheet. Put the chicken in the bread "basket" and bake for 20 minutes, uncovered, at 350°.

Church Builder "Chicken" Salad for Large Groups

This is a "chicken" salad made by members of the All Saints' Episcopal Church in Rehoboth Beach, Delaware, and used at their famous Christmas Shop in October. If you haven't been to this event, GO! Many people think it's the best Christmas Shop on the eastern seaboard.

The chicken salad is one of the best, too. It is, however, made of baked turkey breasts and contains several surprising ingredients. All measurements are necessarily vague. You may vary to taste. Turkey breasts range from 12 to 15 pounds. A 14-pound breast will make enough salad to serve at least 15 people. For small groups, you may use chicken breasts.

Turkey or chicken breasts
Mayonnaise and Miracle Whip
Sugar
White pepper
Celery (about 1 part chopped celery to 4 parts turkey)
Seasoned salt (the church uses McCormick's Salt and Spice)

Bake turkey breasts, following directions on package. Cool and cut into cubes. If using chicken breasts, simmer the chicken in water until done. Cool, and cut into cubes.

Mix a combination of mayonnaise and Miracle Whip, using enough to coat the turkey or chicken pieces well. Add a scant amount of sugar to taste and the celery. Add, if desired, chopped scallions. (The church doesn't use these.) Season with the salt and pepper.

Capital Chicken Casserole

(National first-place winner)

Serves 4

 1 broiler-fryer chicken, cut in parts
 4 tablespoons butter
 1 tablespoon cooking oil
 1 package (8 ounces) fresh mushrooms, sliced
 1 tablespoon flour
 1 can (11 ounces) cream of chicken soup
 1 cup dry white wine
 1 cup water
 ½ cup cream
 1 teaspoon salt
 ¼ teaspoon tarragon leaves
 ¼ teaspoon pepper
 1 can (15 ounces) artichoke hearts, drained
 6 green onions, green and white parts included, chopped
 2 tablespoons chopped parsley

In large fry pan, heat butter and oil to medium temperature until butter melts. Add chicken and cook about 10 minutes or until brown on all sides. Remove chicken and place in baking pan or casserole. In same fry pan, sauté mushrooms about 5 minutes or until tender. Stir in flour. Add soup, wine and water; simmer, stirring, about 10 minutes or until sauce thickens. Stir in cream, salt, tarragon and pepper; pour over chicken. Bake, uncovered, at 350° for 60 minutes. Mix in artichoke hearts, green onions and parsley. Bake about 5 more minutes or until fork can be inserted in chicken with ease.

Chicken and Asparagus Casserole

(Delmarva first-place winner)

Serves 4

2 whole broiler-fryer chicken breasts, skinned and boned, and sliced into 2-by-4½-inch pieces

1½ teaspoons MSG

¼ teaspoon pepper

½ cup corn oil

2 packages frozen asparagus

½ cup mayonnaise

1 teaspoon lemon juice

½ teaspoon curry powder

1 cup shredded Cheddar cheese

After cutting up chicken, sprinkle it with the MSG and pepper. Pour the corn oil into a 10-inch frying pan. Add chicken and sauté slowly about 6 minutes, or until white and opaque. Remove and dry on paper towels. Cook the asparagus by package directions. Drain. Place asparagus on bottom of shallow baking pan. Place chicken over asparagus. Mix together the mayonnaise, lemon juice and curry powder. Pour over the chicken and asparagus. Sprinkle the cheese on top. Cover with aluminum foil. Bake in a preheated, 375° oven for 30 minutes.

Chicken Dinner in a Soup Bowl

(Delmarva first-place winner)

Serves 4

1 broiler chicken and giblets
Water
2 envelopes chicken-flavor
broth mix
2 stalks chopped celery
1 sliced carrot
3 sprigs parsley
1 teaspoon salt
1 teaspoon Accent

Place chicken and giblets in a large cooking pot and barely cover with water. Add remaining ingredients. Cover and simmer 40 minutes. Remove chicken. Separate meat from bones and skin. Cut in large, bite-sized pieces. Strain broth, and skim off all fat.

Re-heat broth in a 4-quart pot. Add:

1 small head cabbage, cut in
8ths
8 small onions

Cover and cook 20 minutes. Add:

4 carrots, sliced
2 stalks celery, chopped

Cook 10 minutes. Add:

1 cup frozen peas
1 tablespoon margarine
Cut up chicken

Heat for 5 minutes. Serve in a soup plate.

Chicken Korma

(Delmarva first-place winner from Maryland)

Serves 4

8 broiler-fryer chicken thighs, skinned

1 carton (8 ounces) plain yogurt

2 teaspoons curry powder

1 teaspoon salt

1 teaspoon ground coriander

1 teaspoon minced fresh ginger (Use ¼ teaspoon powdered ginger if fresh not available)

4 cloves garlic, minced

½ teaspoon ground red pepper

½ teaspoon lemon juice

2 tablespoons shortening

1 medium onion, chopped

1 large tomato, peeled, chopped

2 bay leaves

In deep bowl, make marinade by mixing together yogurt, curry powder, salt, coriander, ginger, garlic, red pepper, and lemon juice. Add chicken, turning to coat. Cover and let stand at room temperature for 30 minutes. In fry pan, heat shortening to medium temperature. Add onion and cook, stirring, about 5 minutes or until light brown. Stir in tomato and bay leaves; cook 5 minutes. Add chicken and marinade mixture to contents of fry pan and mix thoroughly. Cover and simmer over medium heat, stirring frequently, for about 30 minutes or until fork can be inserted in chicken with ease. Serve over hot cooked rice.

Fried Chicken Salad

(National second-place winner)

Serves 4

2 whole chicken breasts, halved, boned, skinned, and cut into ½-inch strips

¾ cup biscuit mix, divided ¼ and ½

½ teaspoon salt

⅓ cup milk

½ cup cooking oil

4 cups torn pieces fresh spinach

1 cup Mandarin oranges, drained

1 cup cauliflower flowerettes

½ cup sliced celery

⅓ cup walnuts, coarsely chopped

½ teaspoon seasoned salt

½ cup bottled vinegar and oil dressing

In small shallow bowl, mix ¼ cup of the biscuit mix and salt. Add chicken, a few pieces at a time, dredging to coat. In small bowl, make batter by mixing the remaining ½ cup of the biscuit mix and milk. Dip floured chicken pieces in batter to coat. In fry pan, heat oil to medium temperature. Add chicken and cook, turning, about 10 minutes or until brown and a fork can be inserted in chicken with ease. Drain chicken. In large bowl place spinach, oranges, cauliflower, celery, walnuts, seasoned salt and the drained chicken strips; mix together. Add vinegar and oil dressing; toss lightly.

Chapter 10

DELMARVA'S CORNUCOPIA OF VEGETABLES

Question: What food product, thoroughly familiar to every Delmarvan, contains twice as much protein as cheese, three times the protein of meat and fish, four times the protein of eggs, and at the same time reduces fat and cholesterol intake?

Answer: Flour or oil made from the soybean, a crop which covers a large part of Delmarva.

Maybe you have never cooked up a pot of soybeans. Nevertheless, you undoubtedly eat soybean protein all the time. Soy proteins are used in bread, cereal, crackers, cookies, dairy products, luncheon meats, sausage, bacon, frankfurters, beverages, soups, sauces, and baby foods, just to name a few examples. Soybean oil comprises three-quarters of all margarine, two-thirds of the salad and cooking oils, and half the frying and baking fats used in food preparation in America today. This lowly bean is high in poly-unsaturates and costs relatively little.

For 4,000 years the Chinese have been eating soybeans—"Oriental meat." Americans, however, tend to look down at, for instance, hamburger made with soybean meal as an extender. But even if you think such ground meat is "ersatz," the fact is that it's probably a lot better for you than pure ground beef.

If the soybean has so many virtues, how come we aren't eating more of it? Well, probably because soybean use is quite new in the United States. The beans were first introduced here as a hay crop in 1800. It took 60 years for them to become a commercial crop. Now they represent America's top cash commodity for farmers, and they are a vital protein source not only for humans, but also for livestock and poultry.

Only 25 companies in the United States process soybeans. Two of these are on Delmarva—Townsend's Inc. and Perdue, both big chicken producers. Cargill in Norfolk is also a soybean processor. Perdue processes the beans mainly for use as chicken feed. Townsend's uses about half its processed beans for feeds, and sells the other half. Last year, Townsend's processed 12 million bushels of soybeans.

There now exists a National Soybean Processors Association (NSPA) with headquarters in Washington, D.C. Every year, representatives from the 25 U.S. processors meet to discuss what's new in the field. One red hot issue is how to develop lower international trade barriers so that foreign producers of soybean meal and oil do not have an unfair competitive advantage.

"We process the crop the whole world wants," says NSPA. Certainly that is true more and more every year. As the population continues to explode the world needs ever greater amounts of human food, as well as nourishment for livestock and poultry.

You might try a baked soybean casserole (see recipes) that tastes a lot like Boston Baked Beans. There are also many other ways of using this valuable food. The *New York Natural Foods Cookbook* lists 32 soybean recipes, from puddings to bread to mayonnaise to salad to patties. The list doesn't include such delectable items as omelets with soybean sprouts, recipes using soy sauce, or the dozens of other ways soy can be used. The *Joy of Cooking* also contains a number of recipes for soybeans. As that book's author, Irma Rombauer, says, "Soybeans combine well with cheese, tomatoes, onions, and other vegetables. They really need an uplift, being rather on the dull side, but (like some of our friends) respond readily to the right contacts."

So, as you drive around Delmarva, look fondly on all those acres of soy. Much of your next year's eating may well be growing there. That is, it will be growing on land that isn't devoted to wheat, rye, sweet potatoes, white potatoes, melons, brussel sprouts, broccoli, spinach, green beans, lima beans, asparagus, pumpkins, cauliflower, tomatoes, peppers, blueberries, strawberries, apples, peaches, and other manna from Delmarva.

Serves 4

1 pint whipping cream

3 egg yolks

1 cup cracker meal

½ teaspoon salt

3 egg whites, beaten stiff

1 cup cooked carrots mashed
   fine

1 tablespoon butter, melted

Whip cream, beat 1 egg yolk at a time and add to cream. Then add cracker meal, salt, whites of eggs beaten stiff, and carrots. Mix all together and pour into large ring mold over melted butter. Set in pan of hot water and bake in hot oven 30 minutes. Serve with creamed crab in center of ring mold. Or you may fill the center of the ring mold with tender green peas or baby lima beans.

Recipe from *Maryland's Way*.

To Cook Soybeans

To cook soybeans, first place washed and picked-over beans in a bowl large enough to allow the beans to expand three times. Cover them with water. Add a little salt, if desired. Soak all day or over night. Place beans and the same water in a large, heavy kettle. Add extra water, if necessary. Add salt if needed. Simmer for 3 to 4 hours or until the beans are tender. Check during the cooking time to see if more water is needed.

Baked Soybeans

Serves 4

2 cups cooked soybeans and cooking liquor

1 to 2 large chopped onions

¼ pound salt pork

Hot water

1 tablespoon bacon drippings

2 tablespoons dark molasses

1 teaspoon salt, or to taste

½ teaspoon mustard (dry)

2 or 3 tablespoons catsup

Combine beans, onions, bacon drippings, and catsup. Place in a bean pot or covered casserole. Combine molasses, salt, mustard and enough hot water to make 1 cup. Pour the mixture over the beans. Add enough cooking water to cover beans. Place bits of salt pork over the top. Bake covered in a very slow (250°) oven 6 to 8 hours. If the beans look dry while cooking, add a little vegetable or meat stock or some more of the bean water. Use the same as you would Boston Baked Beans.

Delmarva Corn Custard

Serves 4

¼ cup sugar

2 tablespoons flour

3 eggs, beaten

1 can (16 ounces) cream-style corn

1 can (5.3 ounces) evaporated milk

1 tablespoon butter or margarine

Mix together sugar and flour. Stir beaten eggs into flour mixture. Add corn and evaporated milk, mixing well. Pour into greased oven-proof dish. Dot with butter or margarine. Bake at 350° for 40 to 45 minutes, or until knife inserted in center of custard comes out clean.

From *An Eastern Shore Sampler*, prepared by Delmarva Poultry Industry, Inc.

Delmarva Meal in a Bowl

You start with what is referred to on the Peninsula as "a messa lima beans." This means 8 to 12 pounds in the shell, or about 2 quarts shelled limas. It also means large, or Fordhook limas. Baby limas are called "factory beans" on Delmarva, because Delmarvans think they are good only for canning. Big green limas are also called butter beans. In addition, there is a third kind of lima called pole beans, and they are gorgeous if you can get them. Regular limas are bush beans.

Serves 6 to 10

2 quarts shelled lima beans
Water
1 slice salted side meat or fat back
Salt to taste
Sugar to taste
2 potatoes, peeled and chopped
2 tomatoes, peeled, seeded, and chopped
Kernels from 2 or 3 ears of corn

Put beans in a big pot with water and side meat. There should be enough water to cover the ingredients. Add tomatoes, salt, sugar, and potatoes. Simmer about 2 hours. Add more water if necessary. Ten minutes before serving, add corn kernels. Serve in a bowl with the broth on a warm summer day with hot biscuits, iced tea, and cantaloupe for dessert.

This dish is closely related to Succotash, which is an Indian dish that was picked up by the early European settlers.

Nowadays, many people think vegetables should be steamed or cooked only a little while. Nevertheless, this is a delicious way to make vegetables into the main dish of a meal. And don't forget, you're eating the broth, too, so none of the vitamins is lost.

Recipe courtesy of Evelyn Thoroughgood.

Eastern Shore Sauerkraut Baked with Apples

Serves 4 to 6

6 medium apples

2 tablespoons brown sugar

1 onion

2 cups sauerkraut, canned or fresh

Pare, core, and slice apples; mix sugar through them. (More sugar may be needed if apples are very tart.) Chop onion fine, mix with apples and sauerkraut, and put all in a buttered baking dish. Cover and cook at 350° for 2 or 3 hours, the longer the better. Do not let it get dry, and stir occasionally. Uncover for the last half hour of baking. The apples must be the kind that will cook up soft. In a pinch, the same amount of applesauce can be used.

Recipe from *Maryland's Way*.

Fresh Broccoli Bake

Here's a new broccoli idea. It comes from the ties around a bunch of broccoli marketed under the name of "Andy Boy."

Serves 6

1 three-ounce package cream cheese

1½ cups milk

2 eggs, beaten

1 tablespoon lemon juice

½ teaspoon salt

¼ teaspoon nutmeg

1 tablespoon chopped parsley

3 cups cooked broccoli

Blend the cream cheese and milk. Add the remaining ingredients. Pour into a well-buttered loaf pan. Bake at 325° for 1 hour.

Note: A little garlic powder and some chopped green onions are good tastes to add while you are preparing this vegetable dish.

Frozen Cucumbers

**Makes approximately
sixteen ½-cup servings**

8   cups thinly sliced unpeeled
    cucumbers

1½ tablespoons salt

1   medium onion, thinly sliced

½   cup vinegar

1½ cups sugar or less

Mix salt with cucumbers and onion, cover, and refrigerate for 2 hours. Drain off juice, getting out as much as possible, but do not rinse. Mix sugar and vinegar and stir to dissolve sugar. Pour over cucumbers and onion; place in small containers and freeze. Cucumbers can be thawed and eaten any time.

Recipe from *An Eastern Shore Sampler* prepared by Delmarva Poultry Industry, Inc.

Green Pea "Soup"

This recipe is another longtime, summertime favorite with country folk. Church suppers often serve this, and you can find it in many small restaurants that feature home-style farm cooking.

The dish isn't actually a soup, nor are there really any recipes written down for it. You'll have to taste your way along.

Pick or buy a "messa" green peas. (This means about 4 to 6 pounds, or enough to make about 1 quart of shelled peas.) Cook them in a heavy pan with enough salted water to more than cover the peas. Some people add to the peas scrubbed baby white potatoes and butter. Others add bits of salt pork and tiny slippery dumplings. There are also those who favor very small drop dumplings. Take your choice. Whichever you choose, cook the whole thing for about half an hour, or until everything's done. Ladle the result into a soup bowl and have it for lunch. On a hot summer day, crab salad is a wonderful accompaniment, they say.

Old-timers don't hold with modern quick cooking or steaming of vegetables. "They cook 'em to death," one Delmarvan said. On the other hand, they don't throw the vegetable water away, so all the vitamins are left in.

Mary Bolton's Recipe for Giant-Size Zucchini

Given a little August heat wave, zucchinis on the Peninsula begin to act as if they were watermelons. One day, these squashes are the size of the small, manageable vegetables you buy in grocery stores. The next day, they explode into enormous balloon-like objects, 15 to 20 inches long and 4 to 5 inches in diameter.

You might think that vegetables of such magnitude would be stringy and bitter. Not a bit of it! Sweet as honey and very tender. Slicing them, however, produces slabs as big as butter plates. Hardly "ray-feened." Don't despair. Try this recipe.

A 15-inch long, 4 inch in diameter zucchini serves 4 to 6

1 large zucchini
Salt and pepper to taste
1 egg, slightly beaten
⅓ cup cottage cheese
1 cup shredded Cheddar cheese
Fresh or dried chopped parsley and chives if desired

Simmer the whole zucchini until tender. (For huge ones, use a roasting pan.) Zucchinis cook quickly and should not be cooked too long or they get all squishy and unflavorful. Most zucchinis should take only 1 to 2 minutes of cooking, either when boiled or steamed. Cool. Slice in half lengthwise. Scoop out the seeds. Sprinkle zucchini with salt and pepper. Mix together egg, cottage cheese, Cheddar cheese, parsley, chives, and more salt and pepper. Spread this mixture in the cavities. Bake 15 minutes at 350°, then turn oven to 450° for a few minutes until the stuffing is brown and bubbly. Delectable!

Norn Lee's Hopping John

Delmarva custom has it that for luck you should always eat black-eyed peas on New Year's Day. "Peninchulans" also think that the first guest on New Year's should be a man, and that he should arrive with black-eyed peas in hand.

Serves 4 to 6

1 can cooked black-eyed peas

2 big onions

1 or 2 chili peppers

¼ pound salt pork or bacon

1 cup rice

1½ cups water

Salt and pepper to taste

Fry the onion and red peppers flavored with salt and pepper. Add cooked peas, pork, uncooked rice, and water. Boil 8 minutes, stirring twice. Let stand 35 minutes with heat turned off.

In this era of mouthwash and deodorant, much as been made about the evil effects of onion eating. Richard Armour wrote:

The onion eater and his brother,
Though inoffensive to each other,
Are by their diet alienated
From those who've not participated.

On the other hand, the flavor of an onion cannot be duplicated by any less pungent bulb. One might comment, therefore:

Said Onion One to Onion Two,
"I don't believe all this to-do
About our making folks say 'Phew!'
It must be rumor, quite untrue.

"Why should our presence in a stew
Or on a spitted barbecue
Or even in a French ragout
Make us so socially taboo?

"It seems to me they should extol
Us, knowing that it's not our goal
To play this alienating role
In casserole or salad bowl!

"And if our flavor they'd eschew
They'd miss us when they said 'Adieu,'
For, let me add, quite *entre nous*
I think our smell is nice, don't you?"

As somebody said, "Practically every recipe I know begins with 'Chop an onion, and fry it until golden brown.'" Some onion recipes are so

good you don't care if they ruin you socially. And remember this:
People have been cultivating and eating onions ever since recorded
history began, and it doesn't seem to have delayed the population
explosion.

So, as the poet wrote:

Let onion atoms lurk within the bowl
And, scarce suspected, animate the whole.

Onion Pie

Serves 6 to 8

4 to 5 pounds onions, peeled
and sliced

1 tablespoon butter or
margarine

2 tablespoons water

¼ pint whipping cream (not
whipped)

Enough biscuit dough or
pie dough to cover a 10-
inch pie pan

Cook onions slowly in a covered frying
pan with butter or margarine and water.
This should take about half an hour.
Check frequently, adding more margarine or water if necessary.

When onions are done, put them in
a buttered deep dish 10-inch pie pan.
Cover with whipping cream. Top with
biscuit or pie dough. Bake the pie at 425°
for about 25 minutes.

Not very thinning, but delicious.

Fried Parsnips

Parsnips are a neglected vegetable, a status they in no way deserve. These cold weather relatives of carrots are ancient herbs, having been cultivated long before the Christian era. It is said that the Emperor Tiberius, a real gourmet, used to have parsnips imported from areas along the Rhine so that he might enjoy this taste treat.

All those generations of parsnip eaters can't have been wrong. So rise above Parsnip Prejudice. Try the following.

Peel parsnips with vegetable peeler. Cook until just soft in salted water. Slice lengthwise into strips ¼-inch thick. Sauté in margarine until golden brown on both sides.

Two of Pat Bonk's Favorite Vegetable Recipes

The Draper King Cole Company in Milton, Delaware, processes vegetables which are shipped all around the country under 800 labels. In addition to canning or freezing many other kinds of vegetables, Draper King Cole is the biggest potato processor in the United States, and packs one-third of all the nation's carrots.

Harry Bonk is Chairman of the Board of this busy company. Pat Bonk, Harry's wife, loves to cook. Here are two of her favorite recipes.

Potatoes Au Gratin

Serves 6

2 cans sliced potatoes ("'King Cole' natch," Pat writes.)

2 tablespoons butter or margarine

1½ teaspoons salt

½ teaspoon Worcestershire sauce

Dash black pepper

½ cup sharp Cheddar cheese, grated

2 tablespoons parsley

¼ cup chopped onion

½ cup half and half cream

Place potatoes in shallow baking pan. Dot with butter. Sprinkle with remaining ingredients, except cream. Pour cream over potatoes. Bake at 350° for 45 minutes.

Pickled Carrots

Serves 12 to 14 at a buffet

3 one-pound cans (6 cups) sliced carrots

1 large onion, sliced

1 green pepper, sliced

1 can tomato soup

½ cup salad oil

1 cup sugar

¾ cup vinegar

1 teaspoon mustard

1 teaspoon Worcestershire sauce

1 teaspoon salt

Drain canned carrots well. Mix soup, oil, sugar, vinegar, and mustard. Heat mixture to dissolve sugar. Cool. Add carrots, onions, and peppers. Serve cold.

Baked Tomato Casserole

Serves 4 to 6

5 or 6 chopped tomatoes or one 29-ounce can tomatoes

2 tablespoons chopped onion

2 tablespoons chopped green pepper

½ to ¼ stick melted butter or margarine

½ cup brown sugar

2 pieces bread broken into small bits

Salt and pepper to taste

Mix all ingredients in an iron skillet or heavy casserole. Bake slowly at 250°, 2 to 3 hours, or cook very slowly on top of stove. The end result should be a deep brick-red color.

Chapter 11
BREADS AND OTHER STARCHY TEMPTATIONS

Many Delmarvans think that a meal without bread, particularly hot bread, "ain't fittin to be called a meal a tall." The cornmeal breads are particularly loved. American Indians, to whom we owe a great corn bread debt, got flour by grinding kidney and pinto beans as well as corn, and their breads often contained both kinds of flours.

The Indians also made an equivalent of blueberry and cranberry muffins. Sweet potatoes were made into bread, biscuits, and desserts. Wild honey and maple sugar were added to cornmeal mush to make sweet dishes.

Many Indians lived on the Peninsula. All of them belonged to the great Algonquian family spread across the middle and southern part of the eastern United States. Some tribe names such as Lenape, Lenni, Nanticoke, Choptank, Wicomico, Pocomo, Assateague, Chincoteague, and Powhatan are still in use today as place names.

The Indians enjoyed all the Delmarva foods mentioned here. They also hunted bears and wild turkeys, as well as the other small animals which are still found on the Peninsula. Indians developed the log canoes used in fishing and racing today.

Indians still live on the Peninsula. A particularly active and ethnic-conscious group of Nanticokes lives on the Indian River near "O-Korchard." This tribe holds a big pow-wow every year, to which visitors are welcomed.

So next time you bite into steaming hot corn bread dripping with butter, think kindly on the Indians who introduced your ancestors to this ambrosia.

Bishopville Church Supper Corn Pone

Serves 4 to 6

2 cups white cornmeal

½ cup flour

1 cup sugar

1 teaspoon salt

3 cups water

1 stick margarine

1½ cups cold milk

3 eggs, slightly beaten

Mix cornmeal, flour, sugar, and salt in a big bowl. Heat together the water and margarine. Pour water and margarine over the dry ingredients. Mix. Add milk and eggs, continuing to stir. Pour into greased, 9-by-13-inch sheet-cake pan. Bake at 400° for 45 minutes to 1 hour.

Recipe courtesy of Janet Scott.

Country Dish Using Corn Pone

Pork sausage

Apples

Corn pone

Cook sausage in frying pan until done. Remove sausage and drain. Remove cores from apples, cut into 8ths and fry in sausage grease. If apples are tart, sprinkle a little sugar over them as they are cooking. Remove apples. Pour off excess grease. Break corn pone into small pieces. In frying pan, mix together sausage, apples, and pone. Reheat gently, and serve. In Delmarva kitchens, the proportions of apples, sausages, and pone vary according to how much of each is on hand. Even amounts of each is a satisfactory formula.

This old recipe comes from Hannah Mary Burton via Comfort Marvil. Hannah Mary Burton and her family worked for generations for the Burton family of Lewes, Delaware. After Hannah Mary Burton moved to the country, she used to come into town weekly, driving a horse and rubber-tired wagon, to sell her pone, home-raised squabs, and other goodies.

Comfort Marvil was active in the promotion of interest in Lewes history. She helped in the restoration of some of the houses in the Lewes Historical Society complex, an interesting feature of this old (1631) town. Comfort's husband, Dr. James Marvil, founded the Lewes Historical Society, one of the most active historical groups in the state.

This recipe calls for New Orleans molasses, which is lighter and has a greater sugar content than the rummy-flavored Puerto Rico molasses. If you don't have New Orleans molasses on hand, nor an iron "Dutch oven," nor yet an oven in a "wood cook-stove," refer to the Bishopville Church Supper Corn Pone recipe and cook the pone in a heavy pan at 400° for 45 minutes to 1 hour. You might also note that the Bishopville recipe includes butter and eggs, an addition considered heresy by corn pone purists.

Cold water
4 quarts sifted cornmeal
½ cup New Orleans molasses
¼ cup sugar
1 tablespoon salt
1 cup flour

Add enough cold water to cornmeal to make a soft batter. Scald well, mashing the lumps. Add New Orleans molasses, sugar, salt, and flour. Grease Dutch oven well, and put in pone mixture. Put in oven of wood cook-stove and let bake from 5 to 6 hours with a good fire. Then open your stove and let the pone remain until morning. Before you go to bed, or about eleven o'clock, put another stick of wood on.

Serves 4

1 cup macaroni,
  preferably elbow
1½ cups milk
1 stick butter or
  margarine
1 cup soft bread crumbs
1 teaspoon salt
1 tablespoon chopped
  green pepper
1 tablespoon chopped
  parsley (optional)
1 small jar chopped
  pimiento (optional)
1 tablespoon chopped
  chives
1½ to 2 cups grated Cheddar
  cheese (half mild, half
  sharp)
2 eggs slightly beaten

Cook macaroni 15 minutes. Drain. Scald milk and add the butter to the milk. Cool. Pour into large bowl in which the eggs have been beaten. Add the bread crumbs, salt, green pepper, parsley, chives, and pimiento. Add grated cheese and the macaroni.

Place in a buttered 9-by-5-inch loaf pan or a 1½-quart casserole. Place dish in a pan of water, and bake at 350° for about an hour. If doubling the recipe, cook about 1 hour and 15 minutes.

Serve with a tomato sauce. This could be thickened tomato juice or V-8 juice. In a pinch, undiluted canned tomato soup can be used. Add to it some chopped chives and a tablespoon or so of butter.

The loaf looks prettiest when turned onto a platter, with a little of the sauce on top and parsley around it.

Note: Hattie, whose recipe this is, was my mother, Hattie Bishop Marvin. This was her favorite dish to serve at bridge club luncheon parties. In summer the ladies ate at card tables set up in the flagstoned grape arbor, and the menu often included green peas (shelled that morning), hot baking powder biscuits with butter and jam, pickles, olives, and fruit salad. Dessert was homemade ice cream, peach or strawberry, and with it cookies or cake. After lunch, the women all played bridge, though it is a mystery how the players were able to stay awake after that anything-but-light lunch.

Hattie's White Bread

This is just about the best white bread "you'll ever put in your mouth."

Makes 2 to 3 loaves of bread

1   yeast cake

2   tablespoons warm water

1   teaspoon sugar

2   cups of milk

2   eggs, slightly beaten

1   tablespoon salt

3   tablespoons sugar

3   tablespoons butter

    Flour

Melt yeast cake in warm water and sugar. Scald milk. Cool slightly. Pour over eggs, salt, and sugar. When mixture is lukewarm add the yeast and enough flour to form a soft lump. Knead on a floured board. Place dough in a greased large bowl. Cover with a tea towel and let rise in a warm place for 2 to 3 hours.

Knead again on a very lightly floured board, adding butter. Return to bowl. Cover again with tea towel. Let rise 1 more hour.

Knead again, this time on an unfloured board, if possible. The less flour you use, the better will be the bread. Cut into two loaves. Shape slightly and place in buttered bread pans. At this point, the bread dough should fill about half the pan. If you have more dough than this, make an extra small loaf. Brush tops of loaves with melted butter. Cover with tea towel, and let rise until twice the size. Bake in a 350° preheated oven for about 40 minutes, or until loaves seem loose in the pans. Turn out on rack, and cool some before cutting.

If you wish, you may place the dough in the refrigerator after the first kneading. It will take 3 to 4 hours for the second rising if dough is refrigerated. Without refrigerating the dough, you can start the bread mid-morning and have it ready for evening dinner.

You may also use this recipe for Parker House rolls. After the third kneading, roll dough to a thin sheet, spread melted butter over it, cut with a biscuit cutter, fold, and place, without crowding, on a greased pan. Let rolls rise 2 to 3 hours or until double in size. Bake in preheated 350° oven for 25 minutes.

Whichever method you use, this recipe is guaranteed to produce exclamations of delight both during the baking and the eating.

Jane Rives's Batter Bread

Serves 4

2 cups milk
1 cup water
1 cup white cornmeal
1 teaspoon salt
3 eggs, well beaten
Walnut-size lump of butter
(melted)

Heat the milk and water. When it is warm, add, a little at a time, the cornmeal and salt. When mixture thickens, add the eggs and butter. Pour into a 1-quart size greased baking dish. Bake in a 350° preheated oven for 1 hour, or until brown.

Serve anywhere, anytime. This bread is particularly memorable when used for Sunday morning breakfast along with shad roe and bacon.

Mary Bolton's Baked Cheese Grits

The French have *croissants* and *brioches*. They don't know about corn on the cob, however, one of summer's greatest delights. It is also doubtful if they have ever heard of hominy grits, which came to American menus via the Algonquian Indians. (The Indians also gave us popcorn, another American treat denied to Parisians. How do you suppose they get through movies?)

Boiled grits may be eaten unadorned except for a small lake of melted butter filling the indentation at the top of the mounded grits. When you cook them this way, you should store your remaining grits in a small pan, then slice and fry the pieces for next morning's breakfast. My mother used to refer to this preparation as "Grammy Dowell's breakfast food"—whoever "Grammy Dowell" was. I can't find her in the family tree.

For company, or on special occasions, try the following from famous Rehoboth cook Mary Bolton.

Serves 8

2 cups grits

2 eggs, lightly beaten

1 cup grated Cheddar cheese
  Paprika

1 teaspoon Worcestershire sauce

1 cup milk

1 tablespoon butter

Boil grits in 8 cups water with 1 tablespoon salt. (Or go by directions on box.) When grits are done add remaining ingredients, reserving enough cheese to sprinkle on top. Sprinkle with paprika. Bake 1 hour or longer at 325° or 350°. Good served with cold sliced ham.

"Murlin," "Delwur," or "Virginny" Beaten Biscuit

When referring to Beaten Biscuit, the most tactful thing to do is to ignore the state. Bitter arguments can explode over which state can claim credit for this form of the staff of life. The following recipe is from *Maryland's Way*, and is called Maryland Biscuit.

Makes 50 to 75 biscuits, depending on size

- 7 cups flour
- ¾ cup lard
- ½ tablespoon salt
- ½ teaspoon baking powder
- 1½ cups water
- An axe, a sad iron, a hammer, or a strong hand

Mix ingredients together and beat dough with hammer for 30 minutes. Form into small biscuits and prick tops with fork. Bake 20 to 25 minutes at 325°.

There are various ways of beating biscuits. You may use a sad iron, flat of an axe, a hammer, or the heel of your hand. You must beat until dough blisters and is smooth looking. Beat at least 30 minutes, and 45 minutes for company.

Note: After all this, the biscuits are sometimes called "Murlin," "Virginny," or "Delwur" bullets. Some afficionados say that to keep from breaking your teeth on them, the thing to do is sprinkle them with a little water, wrap in foil, and heat them in your toaster oven. Serve with lots of butter.

A woman in Wye Mills, "Murlin," Ruth S. Orrell, has grown famous for her biscuit, and markets her product all over the Peninsula and beyond. People have been known to ship them to friends and relatives in far away places like Japan and the Middle East. So it is apparent that after you acquire the taste for it, beaten biscuit is a real addiction.

Sausage Biscuits

Makes from 50 to 100
biscuits, depending on size

½ pound hot sausage

½ pound sweet sausage

1 pound sharp Cheddar cheese, grated

3 cups dry Bisquick

Cook sausage in deep frying pan, breaking into pieces lightly while it is browning. Drain off excess fat. Remove from heat and stir in cheese with a wooden spoon. Keep stirring until cheese melts. Add Bisquick and stir until smooth.

Cool until dough is easy to handle. Form into small balls about the size of a nickel. Balls will puff slightly when baked, so don't make them too large.

Place balls on an ungreased baking sheet and bake at 400° about 10 minutes. Serve immediately or freeze, reheating in slow oven set at 300°.

What's Cooking in Lewes by Elaine Mitchell.

The name of this cornbread is an example of the variety of names that has been given to pans used for frying food. Both spiders and skillets originally had 3 or 4 metal feet to keep them above an open fire. The shadow cast looked like a spider, hence the name. The word skillet probably comes from an old French word meaning pan (*escuelette*). Delmarvans use both these words. They also say "fry pan." Still others use "frying pan."

Serves 4 to 6

2 cups sour milk or buttermilk

2 eggs

1¼ cup yellow cornmeal

2 level teaspoons soda

1 level teaspoon salt

2 tablespoons melted butter or bacon fat

Mix buttermilk and eggs. Add remaining ingredients. Mixture will be thin.

Pour into a well-greased, 10-inch frying pan or "spider," preferably iron. Bake in a preheated 425° oven for ½ hour or until center of the bread is firm. Serve by cutting in pie-shaped wedges. This is a moist and delicious corn bread.

Sweet Potato Biscuits

Makes 12 biscuits

1 cup flour

3 tablespoons Crisco or other shortening

½ teaspoon salt

1 cup sweet potatoes, boiled and mashed

½ cup milk

4 teaspoons baking powder

Sift dry ingredients. Beat melted shortening into potatoes. Add milk. Add dry ingredients to potato mixture and work dough until smooth. Roll out to ½ inch thickness on floured board. Cut with biscuit cutter. Brush tops with melted butter. Bake on a greased pan in a hot oven, 425°.

Recipe from *Heartland*.

Chapter 12

DESSERTS NOT FOR DIETERS

Jack Spratt, looking over Delmarva recipes, would see quickly how rich they are—plain out-and-out fattening, in fact. Corn pone, batter bread, corn pudding, slippery dumplings, "frahd" chicken and gravy, clam fritters, and imperial crab are all tempting. Satan, in the guise of a Delmarva menu, can also lure you with homemade ice cream, syllabub, strawberry "pah," wine jelly with rich custard and whipped cream, cakes with inch-thick frosting, and other delectables with a seven-digit calorie count.

These, and many other recipes, don't at all fit into the *nouvelle cuisine*, "Slim Jim and Slim Jane" approach to cooking. In our time, the Twiggy image, thin and cadaverous, has conquered the world. Everybody you know is either dieting or guilt-ridden because he isn't. Fortunes are being made by makers of diet pills, by writers of diet books, and by proprietors of fat farms. In print and on the TV screen, there is a constant clamor about cholesterol, the dangers of extra poundage, and high blood pressure. Celery is on the throne. Banana splits are in the doghouse.

In the middle of all this dietetic brouhaha, many Delmarvans happily continue to consume their old-fashioned, high-cal menus— good, solid meals of meat, potatoes, bread, dessert, and hold the salad. Could this point of view, too, be a result of the Peninsula's long isolation? Do Victorian standards of "pleasingly plump," "stylishly stout," and a "fine figure of a man" still hold on Delmarva?

Interesting idea, isn't it? Maybe on the "Peninchula" there remains a culture where women without 18-inch waistlines can still be considered beautiful. This is not to imply that all Delmarvans have inner-tube middles. Many of them, indeed, are skinny as broomsticks.

Nevertheless, Peninsulans still put great store by good food and good living, and have not yet entirely succumbed to "think thin" bigotry.

That theory should calm your caloric conscience when you try any of these dessert recipes.

If you're on a diet, don't even LOOK at this.

Serves 6 to 8

6 egg whites

1¾ cups sugar

¼ teaspoon cream of tartar

Pinch of salt

1 tablespoon vinegar

¾ pound Almond Roca candy, ground in food chopper

1½ pints to 1 quart heavy cream, whipped

Preheat oven to 225°.

Put all ingredients, except Almond Roca and heavy cream, in electric mixer. Beat for 5 minutes, at least, first at medium speed, then at high speed.

Wet a cookie sheet with a little cold water. On it place oiled brown paper. (Wrapping paper and Wesson oil will do.) Using an 8-inch salad plate, trace 2 outlines on the oiled paper with a pencil. Fill in the centers as evenly as possible with the meringue. Place in oven on rack one notch below center division. Bake for 1 hour. Turn off heat and leave for about 20 minutes longer to dry out. Remove and cool.

Loosen with spatula and place one of the meringue layers on a serving plate. Cover it with a layer of unsweetened whipped cream. Cover that with a layer of Almond Roca candy at least ½ inch thick. On top of that spread more whipped cream. Place second meringue on top and cover top and sides of all with whipped cream. When completed, this looks like a layer cake. Sometimes, browned almonds may be sprinkled over top and sides. Chill in refrigerator at least 24 hours.

Recipe of Mrs. J. Bruce Kremer (Rehoboth Beach's Betty Bingham's mother-in-law).

Charlotte Bailey's Pecan Delight

Charlotte Bailey is the wife of the retired rector of All Saints' Episcopal Church in Rehoboth Beach, Delaware. She is also an inspired cook.

Serves 12 to 14 people

2 cups plus 2 tablespoons flour

2 cups sugar

1½ teaspoons soda

1 teaspoon salt

2 slightly beaten eggs

½ cup brown sugar

½ cup chopped pecans

2½ cups (1 large can) drained fruit cocktail

Sift together the flour, sugar, soda, and salt. Add the eggs and the fruit cocktail. Mix until blended. Pour into a greased 9-by-14-by-2-inch pan. Top with the brown sugar and pecans. Bake 1 hour at 325°. Let cool. Cover tightly. Keep at least 24 hours in the refrigerator before serving.

Two Berry Pies

Blueberries and strawberries have long been important crops on Delmarva. Indeed, in the 19th century, a leading citizen of Delaware, John G. Townsend, Jr., was known as the Strawberry King of America. An abundance of both these fruits is still produced on the Peninsula, and during the season you may "pick your own" at greatly reduced costs. But at any time of the year, try these luscious recipes.

Easy and Delicious Blueberry Pie

Serves 6 to 8

4 cups fresh or frozen blueberries

¾ cup water, divided into ½ and ¼

5 tablespoons flour
Pinch of salt

1 cup sugar

1 ten-inch baked pie shell
Whipped cream

Mix together ¼ cup of the water, the flour, and salt. Bring to a boil 1 cup of the blueberries, the sugar and the remaining half cup of water. When the mixture is boiling, add the flour paste and stir gently until mixture thickens. Remove from the stove and cool. Add remaining blueberries. Place in the baked pie shell. Refrigerate. When serving, garnish with sweetened whipped cream.

Fresh Strawberry Pie

Serves 6 to 8

1 cooled 9-inch baked pie shell

1 three-ounce package cream
cheese

1 quart strawberries

1 cup granulated sugar

2 tablespoons cornstarch

1 cup whipping cream

Spread the cream cheese, blended with sufficient cream to soften it, over the bottom of the pie shell. Wash and hull berries, and drain well. Place half of the berries in the pie shell. Mash and strain remaining berries. Bring to a boil and slowly add sugar and cornstarch, which have been mixed together. Cook on low for 10 minutes, stirring occasionally. Cool, then pour over the berries in the pie shell. Place in the refrigerator until very cold. Decorate with sweetened whipped cream before serving.

Recipe from *Maryland's Way.*

Grandmother Morris's Sponge Cake

This recipe is from Coley Townsend's grandmother.

2 cups sugar
4 eggs
2 cups flour
2 teaspoons baking powder
2 teaspoons vanilla
¼ teaspoon salt
1 cup hot milk
4 tablespoons melted butter

In a large bowl, beat together until fluffy 1 cup sugar and 2 of the eggs. Add remaining eggs and sugar, beating constantly. Sift together 3 times the flour and baking powder. Gradually add this to the egg and sugar mixture. Add vanilla and salt. Stir in hot milk and melted butter. Pour into greased and floured pan.

If you use a 10-inch tube pan, bake at 350°. Check at 40 to 45 minutes. Test with straw or cake tester, which should come out clean when cake is done. Continue baking until done.

In a 9-by-13-inch pan, bake at 350° for 40 minutes, using the same method to test for doneness.

Using 8-inch layer pans, bake at 350° for 30 minutes, again testing for doneness.

Cool on rack. Serve plain, filled, with icing, or with whipped cream.

Homemade ice cream is an all time favorite Delmarva dessert. To be authentic, the ice cream should be hand turned in an old-fashioned crank freezer. The "cranker" should know that to get cream with a velvety texture the pace of the cranking should be steady, with no pauses and no speed-ups. He should also be prepared to crank 10 to 20 minutes, or until he feels a "pull," indicating that the cream has thickened. The can should never be more than ¾ full of cream, as the ice cream increases in bulk as it freezes. The surrounding mixture of salt and ice in the freezer should be 3 parts ice to 1 part rock salt. More salt than this makes the cream freeze faster and turns it grainy. The freezer should be packed about ⅓ full with the ice, then layers of salt and ice added until the freezer is full.

A perfect setting for old-fashioned homemade ice cream requires a somnolent summer day, a family gathering at grandmother's house, and an eager child waiting to lick the dasher after it is removed from the frozen cream.

Here is a recipe for vanilla ice cream for a 3-quart freezer.

Vanilla Ice Cream

Makes slightly less than 3 quarts of ice cream, enough to serve 15 to 20 people

2½ cups sugar

2 tablespoons flour

½ teaspoon salt

5 egg yolks, slightly beaten

4 cups milk

1 quart whipping cream, whipped

1 tablespoon vanilla or more to taste

Mix together the sugar, flour and salt. Add egg yolks. Scald milk in double boiler. Add milk to the egg and flour mixture. Add vanilla. Return mixture to the double boiler and cook over hot water 20 minutes, stirring constantly at first, less after mixture has thickened.

Cool. Fold in whipping cream. Let freshly packed freezer stand 3 minutes before pouring mixture into freezing can. Turn over to your favorite "cranker." If there is to be a time span between cranking and eating, remove dasher, cover container tightly, place container again in the freezer and re-pack with additional salt and ice. Cover with newspapers.

Serve topped with chocolate sauce, fresh strawberries, or fresh peaches. Try a little ground peppermint-stick-candy over the chocolate sauce.

Memories of an ice cream like that stay with you throughout your life.

Here are two dessert recipes from two successful party givers. The Vanilla Surprise comes from Elizabeth Faigle. She and her husband, John (Captain U.S.N. Ret.), give memorable dinner parties in their Rehoboth ocean-front house. The Kahlua Ice Cream Pie is a dessert used by an equally well-known Rehoboth party giver, Jim Marshall. He and his mother, Ginny, often entertain gatherings both large and small in their house on Silver Lake. Both recipes are elegant and easy, and both begin with ice cream.

Vanilla Surprise

Serves 8 to 10

½ gallon vanilla ice cream (store bought)

1 small can crushed pineapple

¾ to 1 cup shredded coconut

½ cup chopped walnuts or pecans

1 small jar Maraschino cherries, chopped

Leave the ice cream out of the refrigerator until it is soft but not soupy. Then turn it into a bowl, and add the remaining ingredients. Put the mixture into a freezing container, and pop it back into the freezer.

Kahlua Ice Cream Pie

Serves 8 to 10

1 package Lady Fingers

½ gallon coffee ice cream

1 quart chocolate ice cream

2 heaping tablespoons instant coffee

½ cup Kahlua liqueur

6 ground Heath or Butterfinger bars

1 can chocolate sauce

Whipped cream

Ring a 10-inch spring-form pan with Lady Finger halves standing like sentinels around the edge of the pan. Let the two kinds of ice cream soften, then mix together all ingredients except chocolate sauce. Fill mold. Put the mold in the freezer and let it harden. Spread a layer of chocolate sauce on top. Return to freezer until ready to serve. Just before serving, remove from freezer and spread sweetened whipped cream on top. Plenty calories. Plenty delicious.

Mrs. Fay was the wonderful Scots nurse and babysitter for our newly born daughter, Catherine. Very down to earth, Mrs. Fay. If the weather turned hot, she padded about barefoot, no matter what elegant company was around. Cath adored her, and so did we. She cooked casually but creatively.

Cath is now in her thirties. During all these years, we have never found a dessert to surpass this one.

Serves 8 to 10

Mix together with your hands in a round, ungreased 9-inch cake pan the following:

- 1 cup flour
- ½ cup margarine
- 2 tablespoons sugar

After mixing, pat down, and prick all over with a fork. Bake at 350° for 10 minutes. Meanwhile, mix together the following (except for jam):

- 1 cup chopped walnuts or pecans
- ½ cup brown sugar
- ½ cup coconut
- 2 eggs
- 1 teaspoon baking powder
- 1 teaspoon vanilla
- 2 tablespoons flour
- Pinch of salt
- Raspberry jam

When the baking shortbread has just begun to turn golden, remove it from the oven. Spread raspberry jam over the top. Put above mixture on top of this and bake again for 20 minutes to ½ hour.

You may serve it plain, or gild the mystery cake with a dab of whipped cream.

Try it. You, too, will thank Mrs. Fay.

Delmarva pumpkins, like everything else on the Peninsula, have a personality all their own. Instead of being yellow-orange, Delmarva pumpkins are a glowing, rosy yellow color, almost pink. Eye stopping.

Here is a wonderful pumpkin pie recipe that achieves its own individuality through the addition of sherry.

Serves 6 to 8

1½ cups milk
½ cup cold water
½ cup flour
4 cups mashed pumpkin
½ teaspoon ground mace
1 rounded teaspoon ground cinnamon
½ cup sherry
½ teaspoon ground cloves
1 teaspoon ground ginger
½ teaspoon salt
1½ cups sugar
1 large tablespoon butter
    Grated rind and juice of 1 lemon
3 eggs, lightly beaten

Bring milk to a boil; blend flour with cold water and stir it into the boiling milk. Stir until thickened. Mix in bowl with pumpkin. Add spices and other ingredients. Lastly, add egg. Pour into 10-inch pie shell and bake in a moderate oven (350°) about 1 hour, until pumpkin is set and glazed, and knife inserted in center comes out clean.

Recipe from *Maryland's Way*.

Sheet Cakes

Fund-raising dinners or suppers are a fundamental part of Delmarva life. By this means, enthusiastic volunteers raise money for church, club, the Volunteer "Far" Company, the D.A.R., or what have you. Usually featured as main dishes are "arsters," "frahd" chicken, chicken and "dumplins," roast beef, or barbecued ribs. Just as fundamental to these suppers or bazaars are sheet cakes.

Here is a way to give panache to any sheet cake. Use any white cake recipe, or, if you want, use a white cake mix. Bake the cake in a buttered, shallow pan, 9-by-13-inches. When cake is done, let it cool slightly before removing from pan. Place cake top side up on a rack to complete cooling.

When the cake is thoroughly cool, cover it with white boiled frosting. When that has set, drizzle over the top and sides melted, unsweetened chocolate.

Elegant looking and elegant tasting.

Boiled Frosting

2 cups sugar

1 cup water

2 egg whites at room
   temperature

⅛ teaspoon salt

⅛ teaspoon cream of tartar or a
   few drops of lemon juice

1 teaspoon vanilla

Heat, stirring, the sugar and water, then boil until syrup forms a soft ball when dropped in cold water. Begin to test after 5 minutes. Whip until frothy the egg whites and salt. Add the syrup in a slow, constant stream, whipping all the time. When all syrup is in, add cream of tartar or lemon juice and the vanilla.

Syllabub

Serves 6

1 pint rich cream
½ cup confectioners sugar
1 glass port or dry sherry
1 teaspoon almond extract
   Sponge cake

Whip cream until very stiff, then stir in sugar and wine. Add almond extract. Serve in sherbet glasses, accompanied by sponge cake.

Recipe from *Maryland's Way*.

This is one of Elaine Mitchell's recipes that she got for her cookbook from a cookbook by the First United Methodist Church in Omaha. In her last cookbook, *Delaware Seacoast Cookbook,* published just before she died, Elaine said that this recipe made the editor of the Omaha cookbook, Joan Rowe, famous. Perhaps you, too, will achieve fame when you make this melt-in-your-mouth cookie.

Makes about 10 dozen cookies

Mix together:

1 cup butter or margarine

2 cups sugar

Add:

2 whole eggs

1 cup salad oil

Pinch salt

1 teaspoon vanilla

Sift together:

5 cups flour

2 teaspoons baking powder

2 teaspoons cream of tartar

Mix all ingredients together, using a wooden spoon.

Roll batter into balls about the size of a walnut. Roll each ball in sugar. Flatten with the bottom of a glass dipped in sugar or with a fork. Bake on a greased cookie sheet 10 to 12 minutes in an oven preheated to 350°. Cool on a rack and store in an airtight container.

White Potato Pie

Serves 6 to 8

1 pound "arsh" potatoes

⅔ cup butter

¾ cup sugar

Salt to taste

½ cup heavy cream

½ cup milk

4 eggs

½ teaspoon baking powder

Juice and grated rind of 1 lemon

Season to taste with grated nutmeg, vanilla, or ¼ cup sherry wine

1 pastry shell

Cook potatoes, mashing them through a ricer when done. Add butter to hot potatoes, mixing well. Stir in sugar, salt, cream, and milk, then baking powder, lemon juice and rind, nutmeg and vanilla or sherry. Beat eggs well and stir into potato mixture. Line a 10-inch pie pan with pastry and fill with the mixture. Bake in a moderate (350°) oven for about 1 hour, or until a knife inserted in the filling comes out clean.

Recipe from *Maryland's Way*.

Sweet Potato Pie

This dessert is very popular on Delmarva.

Serves 6 to 8

1 nine-inch unbaked pie shell
2 cups mashed sweet potatoes
2 eggs
¾ cup sugar
¼ cup melted butter
1 teaspoon vanilla
1 teaspoon cinnamon
½ teaspoon salt
½ teaspoon ginger
¼ teaspoon cloves
1⅔ cup evaporated milk

Prepare pastry and refrigerate until ready for filling. Mash sweet potatoes in a large mixing bowl; add melted butter, sugar, cinnamon, salt, ginger, cloves, and mix well with electric mixer. In a small bowl, beat eggs; add eggs and milk or cream to sweet potato mixture, blending thoroughly until mixture is smooth.

Pour into pastry-lined pan and bake 15 minutes in a preheated 425° oven. Reduce oven temperature to 350° and bake 25 to 35 minutes longer, or until knife inserted in center comes out clean. Cool on wire rack. To serve, garnish with sherried whipped cream if desired. (Just add a tablespoon of sherry and a little sugar to 1 cup of whipped cream.)

Recipe from *What's Cooking in Lewes*, by Elaine Mitchell.

Wyetown Strawberry Meringue

Serves 6

6 egg whites

½ teaspoon cream of tartar

¼ teaspoon salt

1½ cups sugar

1 teaspoon vanilla

¼ cup slivered blanched almonds

2 cups strawberries or more

1 cup cream for whipping

Preheat oven to 400°. In a large bowl beat egg whites with cream of tartar and salt until foamy white. Beat in the sugar, 1 tablespoon at a time, beating well after each addition, until meringue stands in firm peaks. The sugar should be completely dissolved before more is added. Fold in vanilla. Spoon meringue into 8-inch buttered, spring-form pan; make a hollow the size of a tablespoon in the middle. Sprinkle slivered almonds over top of meringue. Place in the hot oven, close oven door, and turn heat off immediately. Leave meringue to slow-bake, without peeking, even once, overnight, or at least 12 hours.

Remove meringue from oven. Loosen around edge with knife. Release spring and carefully lift off the side of the pan. Slide meringue onto serving plate. About 1 hour before serving, hull and slice enough strawberries to make 1 cup, adding sugar if necessary. Spoon over meringue. Beat cream until stiff. Spoon over strawberries and chill. Garnish with remaining whole or sliced berries.

Recipe from *Maryland's Way*.

Chapter 13

POT LUCK

If you go in for the esoteric, there are recipe books that will tell you how to cook squirrel (the original meat for Brunswick Stew, which now features chicken), snapping turtle, venison, rabbit, skunk, possum, and other delicacies not too often found on the tables of middle America. All these animals still live in the many woods that decorate Delmarva. Fair numbers of Peninsulans still hunt and eat them.

Because of space, however, this book is limited to just three rarities—"mussrat" stew, barbecued ox, and dandelion wine. The latter two recipes appear in this section. All the recipes in Pot Luck, however, are well worth trying.

Baked Pineapple

Serves 4 to 6

1 can crushed pineapple

2 eggs

¼ pound butter

½ cup sugar

2 tablespoons flour

5 slices bread

Beat eggs. Mix with pineapple, sugar, and flour. Put in buttered casserole. Pour the butter in a frying pan and heat. Cut the bread in small squares. Stir bread in hot butter until brown, taking care not to burn the bread. Heat casserole in the oven for a few minutes. Remove and put browned bread on top. Bake at 350° for about ½ hour. Use in place of a vegetable.

Recipe from *Recipes Old and New* compiled by the Delmar Historical Society.

Barbecued Ox

Harry Bonk runs the King Cole Ranch near Milton, Delaware, which is one of the largest cattle-feeding ranches east of the Mississippi. One year, the Bonks gave a party for a thousand or so people. Guests were served barbecued ox. This dish is also featured at a biennial Delaware event held after elections—Return(s) Day—in Georgetown. Winners ride with losers in horse-drawn carriages; the town crier, dressed in a top hat, announces election results; bands play; and the milling throngs partake of barbecued ox sandwiches. In case you have a cattle ranch, here's a good recipe to follow.

Serves 500 to 1,000, depending on how it's sliced

One 2,300-pound ox

Before "dressing out" ox, prepare a bed of coals covering a 6-by-8-foot area. Let coals burn 3 to 4 hours until they are white. Rake frequently to keep temperature even and low, constantly adding new coals.

Put the ox on a rack over the coals (no easy feat). Have someone turn the ox one-quarter turn every 15 minutes for 20 to 24 hours, and brush the ox with barbecue sauce, using a large paint brush. Serve the sliced meat on warm, buttered rolls. Baked beans, sliced tomatoes, and whiskey sours are good accompaniments.

Blueberry Soup With Dumplings   158

Serves 6 to 8

3 to 4 cups fresh or frozen blueberries

2 cups warm water

4 tablespoons sugar

2 tablespoons cornstarch

Sour cream or whipped cream

Pinch of salt

¼ teaspoon cinnamon

2 tablespoons lemon juice

¼ teaspoon vanilla

½ recipe baking powder biscuits

Combine blueberries with the water and purée in blender. In a saucepan, combine sugar, cornstarch, salt, and cinnamon. Add a little water and stir until smooth. Add purée. Bring mixture to a boil. Simmer until soup becomes thick and clear. Drop biscuit-dumplings by small teaspoonfuls onto the soup. Cover. Cook gently 12 to 15 minutes. When the dumplings are done, stir in the lemon juice and vanilla, taking care not to break the dumplings. Chill. Serve as a soup before a summer salad lunch, or use as a dessert with sour cream or whipped cream.

You may also make the soup into a cobbler by rolling out the biscuit dough to about ⅓-inch thick, pouring the soup into a baking dish, dotting it with butter, and placing the biscuit dough on top. Bake at 425° for 20 to 25 minutes.

Comfort Marvil's Beach Plum Jelly

Use 2/3 ripe plums to ⅓ green plums. Plums should be picked during the third week in August. Wash. Put in heavy kettle. Add water to half cover the plums. Boil until the plums split and the stones fall out. Put all in a jelly bag and drain overnight.

Measure liquid and add same amount of sugar. Put in heavy kettle and boil until mixture reaches the jell mark on a jelly thermometer. Do not do more than 4 cups at a time. Put in jelly glasses.

Note: If you do not have a jelly thermometer, use a silver spoon that has been chilled in the refrigerator to dip out a small amount of the jelly. If the liquid forms wrinkles on the top when you blow on it or push it with a knife, it will jell.

Makes about 8 quarts

4 quarts dandelion flowers
4 quarts water
  Rind of 2 oranges
  Grated rind of 1 lemon
¾ cup yeast
4 pounds sugar
  Flesh of 2 oranges

Boil first four ingredients for 20 minutes, then strain. Add the sugar. When mixture has cooled, add yeast. Slice the 2 oranges into the mixture, after having removed the seeds. Let mixture stand in an open vessel 3 or 4 days. Strain, bottle, and cork tightly.

Recipe from an old, hand-written cookbook, courtesy of Ruth Chambers Stewart.

Note: In these old recipes, the yeast mentioned was usually homemade yeast, often concocted from potatoes. It was not as potent as modern brewer's yeast. One yeast cake or 1 packet of yeast will substitute well.

Glazed Bacon Yum Yums

Serves 10 to 20

2 pounds thick-sliced bacon
1½ cups brown sugar
1½ tablespoons dry mustard

Cut bacon into bite-sized pieces with scissors. Place in a single layer in a shallow pan. Combine sugar and mustard. Sprinkle over the bacon. Bake at 250° for 1 hour. Marvelous as an appetizer.

Recipe from *The Country School Cookbook* prepared by the Parents' Association of the Country School in Easton, Maryland, as quoted in *Peninsula Pacemaker*.

Green Pepper Jelly

Makes about 4 eight-ounce jars

6 large green or red sweet peppers cut into small pieces

1½ cups cider vinegar

1 teaspoon crushed red pepper

6 cups sugar

½ teaspoon salt

1 six-ounce bottle liquid pectin

Green or red food coloring

Put half the peppers and half the vinegar into blender and liquefy. Repeat process with remaining peppers and vinegar. Place liquid in a large saucepan. Add the red pepper, sugar, and salt. Bring mixture to a boil and add the pectin. Boil until it thickens when dropped from a spoon—about 20 minutes. (See Beach Plum Jelly for jelling test.) Add a few drops of red or green food coloring. Pour hot jelly mixture into hot, sterilized jars, leaving ½-inch space on top. Adjust caps or cover with paraffin. Serve as a relish with meat or with cream cheese on crackers.

Recipe from *An Eastern Shore Sampler* prepared by Delmarva Poultry Industry, Inc.

Ham Steak with Pan Gravy

Serves 4 to 6, depending on size of ham slices

2   slices ham, ½-inch thick

2   tablespoons butter or margarine

1   tablespoon flour

½   cup water

Pepper, to taste

1   cup milk

Parsley, if desired

Place ham slices in hot water for half an hour. Dry them. Brown lightly on each side in 1 tablespoon of the butter or margarine. Add the water, cover pan, and simmer until ham is tender. Place ham on hot platter and keep warm while you make the gravy. Melt the other tablespoon of butter or margarine in the frying pan. Add the flour and pepper and blend. This mixture should be as thin as light cream. If it is not, add more butter or margarine. Add the milk all at once, stirring until the sauce is smooth and thickened. Pour the sauce over the ham. Garnish with parsley. Good served with fried tomatoes and grits.

Fried Tomatoes

Serves 4

6 green tomatoes or 6 firm ripe
  tomatoes
1 teaspoon salt
¼ teaspoon pepper
3 tablespoons butter or bacon
  drippings
  Flour or fine bread crumbs
  (optional)

Cut tomatoes in ¼-inch slices. Season with the salt and pepper. Slices may be dipped in flour or fine bread crumbs if desired. Melt butter or drippings in a frying pan. Add tomatoes. Brown slowly on one side. Turn. Cook until golden brown. Remove. Remaining juice in the pan should be added to the ham gravy. If tomatoes have been cooked alone, a gravy may be made from the drippings, using the method given in the previous recipe.

Phyllis Seymour's Cranberry Surprise

Makes about 4 jelly jars

1 pound cranberries
2 cups water
2 cups sugar
2 tablespoons any chutney
1 teaspoon curry powder
1 cup chopped walnuts or
  pecans

Cook cranberries in water and sugar. Squash berries as they are popping and cooking. When cranberries are cooked, add remaining ingredients. Put in glass jelly jars with tops. Refrigerate. This makes an unusual relish for holiday dinners, and also provides nice homemade gifts.

Scrapple is one of the delights that have come to Delmarva from the Pennsylvania Dutch. It is made from corn meal and pork. Wonderful brands of scrapple are produced and sold by many companies on the "Peninchula," and afficionados seem to enjoy arguments as to which brand is best. They are all good. You don't realize how good until you travel west or to New England, where scrapple is practically unknown. Some fancy western grocery stores are now advertising that they carry scrapple, but, of necessity, they have to freeze it, which, of course, makes it crumbly and un-scrapplish.

It is customary to serve fried scrapple at breakfast with scrambled eggs, buttered toast, and jam. On the other hand, it is just as customary to eat scrapple with pancakes and syrup. So take your choice.

Similarly, strong opinions are also held as to how to cook it. "Always start to fry scrapple in a cold pan," great Sussex County cook and hostess, Harriet Wilson, used to say. "Cook it slowly, and turn it only once." Other good cooks think you should dip the slices in flour or biscuit mix, then fry them slowly in butter. Scrapple makes for lots of people-scraps, as you can see.

Scrapple also makes a delectable sandwich.

Scrapple and Melted Cheese Sandwich

Fry enough thin slices of scrapple to cover the amount of bread slices you wish to use. When they are done, put them on buttered toast or bread. Cover with thinly sliced cheese. Place in toaster oven until cheese is melted. Remove to plates. Top with mung bean sprouts or chopped lettuce.

Peppers Stuffed with Scrapple

One manufacturer of tasty scrapple is the Kirby and Holloway Company in Harrington, Delaware. These imaginative people came up with this interesting scrapple recipe and the next one (using their own scrapple, of course).

Serves 6

1½ pounds scrapple
3 tablespoons chopped onion
6 large green peppers
1 cup cheese sauce

Cube and soften scrapple over low heat. Add onions. Cut thin slice from stem end of pepper. Remove seeds and plunge in boiling water 5 minutes. Drain and stuff with scrapple. Set peppers in muffin pans. Bake in preheated 350° oven 25 to 30 minutes. Top with cheese sauce. Sprinkle with paprika.

Baked Scrapple with Pineapple—Scrapple Aloha

Serves 6

1 pound scrapple
6 slices of canned pineapple

Grease lightly a shallow baking pan. Arrange pineapple slices in pan. Cut scrapple loaf in 6 pieces. Lay piece of scrapple over each slice of pineapple. Bake at 375° for 35 to 40 minutes, or until scrapple is brown.

More Ways to Use Scrapple for Lunch or Dinner

- Use in place of ham in Eggs Benedict. Call your eggs "Eggs Delmarva."

- Make a sandwich with toasted rye bread, fried scrapple, thin slices of tomatoes, mayonnaise, lettuce, and, if you wish, thin slices of onions.

- Substitute scrapple for the ham in the Maryland Ham Steak and Pan Gravy. Be sure to have fried tomatoes with this.

- Cover fried scrapple with creamed mushrooms.

- Stuff large mushroom caps with scrapple that has already been cooked. Add chopped onions if you want, and mayonnaise or sour cream. Bake 15 minutes at 350°.

Chapter 14
HIGH OCCASIONS

Mark Twain said that part of the secret of success in life is to eat what you like and let the food fight it out inside. Any such interior warfare should immediately call a truce when the officer in charge is enjoying Delmarvalous cooking.

As an example of gracious eating, witness the following menu, and comments thereon, as given in *Maryland's Way*. This was the dinner of The Gourmet Society in 1950, held at the Chesapeake Bay Yacht Club in Easton, Talbot County, Maryland.

Almond Soup
Boned Broiled Shad
Small Cull Soft-Shelled Crabs
Maryland Beaten Biscuit
Boned Squab Chicken
Native Asparagus
Plain Salad with Paté and Ham Flakes in Aspic
Strawberries
Liqueurs
Cigars
Coffee
Fine vintage wines served with each course

"The Soup, the receipt for which was given by Henry James' niece to tonight's impresario, is made from veal shank and/or neck base to which is added the usual ingredients to form a tasty broth, plus pounded almonds and mace. There is no clear record that Henry James ever made or heard of this soup, or that he even liked soup.

"The Boned Broiled Shad is edged with the 'small cull soft crabs' from our host's lower district, Crisfield in Somerset County.

"The famed Maryland Beaten Biscuits were made here in Easton this morning.

"The Plain Salad is accompanied by an aspic, at the bottom of which lies a paté and through which are found flakes of Talbot County raised and cured ham.

"The Strawberries are served with either clotted cream or powdered sugar.

"Hon Edward T. Miller, Host

"Carroll McTavish Elder and Donald Ross, Impresarios

"Saturday, May 13th, 1950"

Don't you wish you'd been there?

And here, from *Maryland's Way*, is a menu for "A Sailing Regatta" that will fill you with visions of the sun and salt breeze of a Delmarva summer.

Crab Feast Ashore

Beer
Coffee
Steamed Crabs
Crab Loaf
Dressed Cucumbers
Corn Roasted in the Husks
Sliced Tomatoes
Mustard Pickle
Salt Sticks
Watermelon

Here is another kind of menu, this one offered by the Eastern Shore of Virginia Chamber of Commerce, which sponsors the annual Seafood Festival in Accomac, Virginia, held on the first Wednesday in May. The heaping plates of fresh goodies from the sea held such great attraction that attendance is now limited to 3,000. Tickets go on sale on October 1st of the year preceding the festival and are usually sold out in one day, so get your request in early. In addition to enjoying the sea breezes and the nearby wild beaches of Assateague Island, here is what you can expect in the way of food.

Clams—Raw, steamed, in fritters, in French fried strips, in broth or in chowder

Oysters—Raw, steamed, or in fritters

Fish—Always local. The species depends on what is being caught. There are always two or three choices, which may include trout, drum, flounder, rock sea squab, or eel.

Accompaniments—Hush Puppies

French Fried Sweet Potatoes

Cole Slaw

Bread, crackers, beverage, pickles, condiments, etc.

Drinks—Beer or soft drinks

Philadelphia celebrated its 300th birthday with tall ships, parades, and other hoopla. During the festivities, however, no mention was made of an old Philadelphia product almost as famous as the city itself—Fish House Punch.

Fifty years after Philadelphia started on its 300-year path, 30 men decided to found a club "for the purpose of more effectively cementing the friendships which have been formed." The formal "cementing" produced the desired result, for, since May 1732, the club, The Schuylkill Fishing Company in the State of Schuylkill, more commonly called The Fish House Club, has been engaged in helping its members enjoy life. It is perhaps the oldest private club in America, and its membership is still limited to 30 men, plus 10 apprentices, from which latter group new members are elected.

The most famous and far-reaching accomplishment of The Schuylkill Fishing Company was the invention of Fish House Punch, an alcoholic nectar which must be the kind of strengthening nostrum consumed by Superman before his every take-off into heroism. The Club has also developed a recipe for Planked Shad, supposed to be delectable, but which can in no way be compared to the potent punch THE PUNCH packs.

The members of the Fishing Company meet every two weeks to drink, dine, and amuse themselves. Apprentices, according to the by-laws, "assist in cooking and serving dinner," and are required to be apprentices "for at least one fishing season."

In pre-Revolutionary days, one gentleman wrote as follows about the club: "There are only Thirty Members, and they have a Governor, a Sheriff, and a Coroner, though God Knows what these Officers do.

"Every Member must Learn how to Cook and Wash dishes, though they have regular cooks. On (a friend's) invitation I went to the Fish House Club Tuesday and Did We Have a Time, Eating, Drinking, Games, Target Shooting, Stage Plays, Singing, All men. No women.

"Before it was half over I did not Know whether I was on foot or horseback. They have a drink there called Fish House Punch.

"It is most excellent if taken in Moderation, but it is so Smoothe that One who does not know its Powers is Likely to take too much.

"I suppose I must have drunk too much of it, but it did not Seem so at the Time. Next Morning was a Difrent Story."

Over 250 years have passed since then, and from all accounts the results are the same. It didn't take any 250 years, however, for the recipe for this renowned concoction to reach Delmarva. "Peninchula" residents have been imbibing this potent ambrosia for as long as anyone can remember.

At the Club, the punch is served in a Lowestoft punch bowl that was presented to the Club in 1812. Originally the recipe called for cube sugar, but it is possible to substitute superfine sugar, which dissolves equally well. Or you may make a simple syrup to guarantee that the sugar is dissolved, in which case you might want to cut down on the amount of sugar and water.

There are dozens of recipes for this punch, all purporting to be the original recipe. Some call for the addition of strong tea, to take the place of some of the water.

In any event, here is one version of the magic ingredients.

Serves 10 to 50, depending on capacity of imbibers

½ cup superfine sugar

2 quarts light rum, or 1 quart light and 1 quart dark

1 quart brandy

¾ cup peach brandy or cordial

2½ cups lemon juice

2 quarts (or less) water

Mix together sugar and a little water. Add rum. Add remaining ingredients.

After you mix it, Fish House Punch needs to sit for at least two hours before being served, so make it well in advance. This also provides a good opportunity to take a taste or two or three to see if the mixture is just right.

We always like to taste and try, don't you?

Ah! Perfect!

As you can see, Fish House Punch is almost straight alcohol, and uses the pallest smossible amount of water. It's the beach prandy which makes the pinsh so droothe and melicious, even though it's streally rong.

To serve the punch, put a barge lock of blice in your Bunch Powl, and more the pixture over it. Then bit sack and lake a sittle tip now and again while gaiting for your wests to arrive.

Rut bemember! Hiss Pounch Fush is deally rynamite! Don't crive your drar after pinking the drunch. Tall a caxi.

Another tittle laste?

Ottoms Bup!

Chapter 15

CODA

Anyone visiting or living on Delmarva (a term of relatively recent coinage) should try to take in some of the annual events which celebrate the area's beauty, history, and abundance. There are waterfowl festivals, poultry festivals, seafood festivals. The wild pony round-up on Chincoteague is famous. So, too, are the house and garden tours. And scattered everywhere are museums presenting the many aspects of life on the Peninsula. No one book can even begin to tell it all.

Washington, Baltimore, Wilmington, and Philadelphia papers often carry stories about upcoming events. Recently, the *New York Times* has run a weekly column on what's happening on the Peninsula. If you are interested in attending a particular event, the best thing to do is to write the Chamber of Commerce of the town involved. If you want to take in special happenings while you are vacationing here, watch the local newspapers to find out when, where, and how much.

It is a unique and fascinating place, Delmarva. As thass how it is up Puckumway on thisseer Peninchula, airywhichaways you look. Mungyew better get raht on down hyear. Jes fer a visit, moind you. They's a awful lotta folk hyear awready.

ACKNOWLEDGMENTS

Thanks are owed to many people for their kind help to me as I was writing this book. My deepest gratitude goes out to them all.

Particularly am I indebted to all the following people and organizations: *The Whale* for letting me use some material from my columns originally published in their fine weekly newspaper; and Elaine Mitchell and her *What's Cooking in Lewes* cookbook, now out of print. (A new one published in 1982 is available at bookstores and at 44 Sussex Drive, Lewes, Delaware.) I am grateful to Bill Dukes, editor and publisher of *Heartland*, a magazine about Delmarva published in Denton, Maryland; to the gracious people associated with *Maryland's Way*, a cookbook available at the Hammond Harwood House in Annapolis, Maryland; to *The Last Resort Cookbook*, now out of print; to Connie Parvis of the Delmarva Poultry Industry, Inc., in Georgetown, Delaware; to the Kirby and Holloway Company of Harrington, Delaware; to Robert Robinson of *The Countian*, Georgetown, Delaware; to Anne Nesbitt, Editor of *Peninsula Pacemaker*, a monthly publication featuring Delmarva events, history, and recipes, published in Seaford, Delaware; to Coley and Susy Townsend; Meredith Jenney; Evelyn Thoroughgood; Ruth Chambers Stewart; Betty Bingham; Pat Bonk; Janet Scott; Elizabeth Faigle; Jim Marshall, and other good cooks who gave me permission to use their recipes; to William Warner, William Tawes, and all the other authors whose writings have enriched everyone's insight and knowledge of the Delmarva Peninsula; and above all to my husband, Ward, and my daughter, Catherine, for all their help and encouragement.